HEART OF DARKNESS

CONTINUUM CHARACTER STUDIES

HEART OF DARKNESS
CHARACTER STUDIES

ASHLEY CHANTLER

continuum

Continuum

The Tower Building   80 Maiden Lane, Suite 704
11 York Road   New York
London SE1 7NX   NY 10038

www.continuumbooks.com

Ashley Chantler has asserted his right under the Copyright, Designs and Patents Act, 1988, to be identified as Author of this work.

British Library Cataloguing-in-Publication Data
A catalogue record for this book is available from the British Library.

ISBN: 978-08264-8174-0 (hardback)
978-08264-9174-9 (paperback)

Library of Congress Cataloging-in-Publication Data
A catalog record for this book is available from the Library of Congress.

Typeset by Servis Filmsetting Ltd, Manchester
Printed and bound in Great Britain by
MPG Books Ltd, Bodmin, Cornwall

CONTENTS

ACKNOWLEDGEMENTS

I would like to thank: David Higgins for his invaluable feedback on an early draft of this book and shining light in the gloom; Lynsey Arnott for her help with the index; the staff of Chester University's library, especially those who dealt with my numerous inter-library loan requests; Anna Sandeman (Continuum) for her support and advice on the first proposal for the series, and her patience when I was completing this book; and Colleen Coalter (Continuum) for her work on the series, gentle reminders and empathy regarding extensions. The proposal for the series was bolstered by supportive quotations from the following, whom I now owe a favour: Annika Bautz, Arthur Bradley, Tracey Cruikshank, Sarah Heaton, Peter Rawlings, Valerie Sanders, Max Saunders, Philip Shaw, and Jim Watt. I am grateful to my colleagues in the Department of English, University of Chester, for the sabbatical that allowed me to get the series and much of the research for this book underway. I must finally thank the following, for various reasons: Derek Alsop, Peter Blair, Gary Calland, Faith Chantler, W. Chantler, Michael Davies, Melissa Fegan, Liam Grest, Robert Riley, Martin Stannard and Chris Walsh.

SERIES EDITOR'S PREFACE

This series aims to promote sophisticated literary analysis through the concept of character. It demonstrates the necessity of linking character analysis to texts' themes, issues and ideas, and encourages students to embrace the complexity of literary characters and the texts in which they appear. The series thus fosters close critical reading and evidence-based discussion, as well as an engagement with historical context, and with literary criticism and theory.

Character Studies was prompted by a general concern in literature departments about students responding to literary characters as if they were real people rather than fictional creations, and writing about them as if they were two-dimensional entities existing in an ahistorical space. Some students tend to think it is enough to observe that King Lear goes 'mad', that Frankenstein is 'ambitious', or that Vladimir and Estragon are 'tender and cruel'. Their comments are correct, but obviously limited.

Thomas Docherty, in his *Reading (Absent) Character: Towards a Theory of Characterization in Fiction*, reminds us to relate characters to ideas but also stresses the necessity of engaging with the complexity of characters:

> If we proceed with the same theory as we apply to allegory [that a character represents one thing, such as Obstinate in Bunyan's *Pilgrim's Progress*], then we will be led to accept that Madame Bovary 'means' or 'represents' some one essence or value, however complex that essence may be. But perhaps, and

more likely, she is many things, and perhaps some of them lead to her character being incoherent, lacking unity, and so on. [. . .] It is clearly wrong to say, in a critical reading, that Kurtz, for example, in Conrad's *Heart of Darkness* represents evil, or ambition, or any other one thing, and to leave it at that; nor is Jude a representative of 'failed aspirations' in Hardy's *Jude the Obscure*; nor is Heathcliff a representation of the proletariat in Emily Brontë's *Wuthering Heights*, and so on. There may be elements of truth in some of these readings of character, but the theory which rests content with trying to discover the singular simple essence of character in this way is inadequate [. . .] (p. xii)

King Lear, for example, is complex, so not easily understandable, and is perhaps 'incoherent, lacking unity'; he is fictional, so must be treated as a construct; and he does not 'mean' or 'represent' one thing. We can relate him to ideas about power, control, judgement, value, sovereignty, the public and the private, sex and sexuality, the body, nature and nurture, appearance, inheritance, socialization, patriarchy, religion, will, blindness, sanity, violence, pessimism, hope, ageing, love, death, grief – and so on.

To ignore this, and to respond to Lear as if he is a real person talking ahistorically, means we simplify both the character and the play; it means, in short, that we forget our responsibilities as literary critics. When, for example, Lear cries, 'Howl, howl, howl, howl! O, you are men of stones!' (5.2.255), it would be wrong to ignore our emotional response, to marginalize our empathy for a father carrying his dead daughter, but we must also engage with such other elements as: the meaning and repetition of 'Howl' (three howls in some editions, four in others); the uncertainty about to whom 'you are men of stones' is directed; what 'men of stones' meant to Shakespeare's audience; the various ways in which the line can be said, and the various effects produced; how what Lear says relates to certain issues in the play and introduces new ideas about being human; what literary critics have written about the line; and what literary theorists have said, or might say, about it.

When we embrace the complexity of character, when we

undertake detailed, sensitive critical analysis that acknowledges historical context, and literary criticism and theory, and when we relate characters to themes, issues and ideas, the texts we study blossom, beautifully and wonderfully, and we realize that we have so much more to say about them. We are also reminded of why they are worthy of study, of why they are important, of why they are great.

Ashley Chantler
University of Chester, UK

INTRODUCTION: AN OVERVIEW OF *HEART OF DARKNESS*

Man goes up river – man meets man – man learns about man.

Simple. But complicated easily. A British man, who is an untrustworthy narrator, writes about when he was once on the Thames with a Director of Companies, a Lawyer, an Accountant and Marlow, a sailor who tells ambiguous stories, who tells an ambiguous and unreliable story about when he was younger and went up the Congo (after visiting Brussels and meeting several troubling people), witnessed the results of European colonialism, responded confusingly to several black people and met a European colonialist, Kurtz, who had given in to unnamed 'lusts', performed 'unspeakable rites' and then died whispering, 'The horror! The horror!', the meaning of which is unclear. Marlow then returns to Brussels, acts like a man who is going insane, and tells a lie, rightly or wrongly, to Kurtz's fiancée. End back on the Thames leaving your readers thinking that even 'Man goes up river' is complicated because the story has suggested that nothing is simple when you think about it.

Conrad knew that the novel was ambiguous. After the first instalment had been published in the February 1899 issue of *Blackwood's Edinburgh Magazine*,[1] he wrote to his friend R. B. Cunninghame Graham: 'There are two more instalments in which the idea is so wrapped up in secondary notions that You – even You! – may miss it' (8 Feb. 1899; Conrad 1986, p. 157). And he pushed for even greater ambiguity when preparing the text for publication in *Youth: A Narrative; and Two Other Stories* (1902): in *Blackwood's*, the story was titled 'The Heart of Darkness', in the 1902 volume as 'Heart of Darkness'.[2] Its ambiguity is one of the many reasons why the novel requires, but also rewards, detailed analysis.

STUDYING *HEART OF DARKNESS*

We tend to dislike ambiguity in literature (and indeed in life) and when faced with it, rather than accepting it, often wield our simplifying critical hammers. But as D. H. Lawrence warns, in his wonderful essay on 'Morality and the Novel' (1925): 'If you try to nail anything down, in the novel, either it kills the novel, or the novel gets up and walks away with the nail' (p. 174).

One way of trying to nail down *Heart of Darkness* is by drawing on Conrad's life and letters. In the introduction of the edition you own there is probably a discussion of Conrad's life as a sailor and what he witnessed in the Congo in 1890. There are probably quotations from his *Congo Diary* (first published in 1925), which details his trek from Matadi to Nselemba (13 June–1 August 1890), and *A Personal Record* (1912, as *Some Reminiscences*), in which he (now famously) wrote:

> It was in 1868, when nine years old or thereabouts, that while looking at a map of Africa of the time and putting my finger on the black space then representing the unsolved mystery of that continent, I said to myself with absolute assurance and an amazing audacity which are no longer in my character now:
> 'When I grow up I shall go *there.*' (Hampson 2000, p. x)

Marlow tells his audience on the *Nellie* that he did the same (pp. 21–2).

Should we then assume that Marlow 'is' Conrad, or at least a fictional spokesperson? Does that help us understand the novel? No, and no. Ignoring the possibility that Conrad was mimicking Marlow (*A Personal Record* was written after *Heart of Darkness*) and never actually did or said those things, it would be critical madness to think that just because a character does a few things that are similar to things the author did then what the character says is the voice of the author. It is also highly reductive. A cursory comparison between Conrad's statement, above, and Marlow's quickly reveals that Conrad's text does not help us understand Marlow's complete statement:

> True, by this time it was not a blank space any more. It had got filled since my boyhood with rivers and lakes and names. It had ceased to be a blank space of delightful mystery – a white patch for a boy to dream gloriously over. It had become a place of darkness. But there was in it one river especially, a mighty big river, that you could see on the map, resembling an immense snake uncoiled, with its head in the sea, its body at rest curving afar over a vast country, and its tail lost in the depths of the land. And as I looked at the map of it in a shop-window, it fascinated me as a snake would a bird – a silly little bird. (p. 22)

If we want to try to get to grips with this complex passage (as I attempt to in Chapter 2), the nine-year-old Conrad is not going to help. We are on our own, to an extent.

Much has been written about *Heart of Darkness*, in fact so much that it can be rather daunting (see the Guide to Further Reading for suggestions on where to begin), and there are volumes of Conrad's letters in which he mentions writing and publishing the novel. Secondary sources (including this one) and letters, though, like autobiographies and biographies, also need to be approached with caution. Letters can give us access to the author, but using them to understand a text is fraught with problems. While completing the three instalments of the novel for *Blackwood's*, for example, Conrad wrote to William Blackwood:

> The title I am thinking of is 'The Heart of Darkness' but the narrative is not gloomy[.] The criminality of inefficiency and pure selfishness when tackling the civilizing work in Africa is a justifiable idea. The subject is of our time distinc[t]ly – though not topically treated. (31 Dec. 1898; Conrad 1986, pp. 139–40)

Should we think that the novel is not 'gloomy' (dark, pessimistic), even if our analysis of it suggests otherwise? Should we ground our discussions of the novel in its representation of the 'criminality of inefficiency and pure selfishness when tackling the civilizing work in Africa', even if we think that the novel's main concern is with epistemological uncertainty, or if we want to consider the presentation of women in the novel? Certainly not. We must also take into account to whom the author is writing. Here, it is to Blackwood, the editor of a conservative, imperialist literary magazine. If Conrad had written, 'The title I am thinking of is "The Heart of Darkness" and the narrative is gloomy. In the light of the death of God thanks to Darwin and Nietzsche, the futility of existence is a justifiable idea', Blackwood might not have printed the story and Conrad would not have got paid.[3]

The early twentieth-century French poet and essayist Paul Valéry reminds us to distance ourselves from the author:

> [I]t can never be too much insisted upon: *there is no true meaning to a text* – no author's authority. Whatever he may have *wanted to say*, he has written what he has written. Once published, a text is like an apparatus that anyone may use as he will and according to his ability: it is not certain that the one who constructed it can use it better than another. Besides, if he knows well what he meant to do, this knowledge always disturbs his perception of what he has done. (p. 152)

In literary studies, the rejection of the author and authorial intention, so giving the reader authority, is encapsulated in the final sentence of a highly influential essay by Roland Barthes: 'the birth of the reader must be at the cost of the death of the Author' (p. 150).[4]

Valéry's 'a text is like an apparatus that anyone may use as he will' and Barthes's promotion of the reader invite anarchy in seminars and written assignments, and it not uncommon for students to say that a text is about whatever we want it to be. 'It's open to interpretation' is a common statement, suggesting that there is no such thing as a wrong reading. They would have difficulty, though, convincing any sane person that *King Lear* is 'about'

George Bush. The play might say something about power and blindness that informs our understanding of Bush, and indeed our understanding of Bush might inform how we respond to Lear, but the play was written at a particular time in history. Furthermore, the words on the page place certain limits on meaning, so on critical interpretation.[5] Using secondary sources can help you work out what the text might mean, to avoid making wild claims in your assignments, but secondary sources should never squeeze out your close reading of the novel. A critic's interpretation is just *their* interpretation; their attempt to nail down the novel might be flawed.

Heart of Darkness was written at the end of a century that had seen a significant change in how people understood themselves and the world. There is not the space here to go into detail (see Ian Watt's *Conrad in the Nineteenth Century* and Cedric Watts's *A Preface to Conrad*), but a few short quotations will give you a sense of what Watt and Watts discuss as late nineteenth-century uncertainty and pessimism. Matthew Arnold's 'Dover Beach' (1867) ends:

> Ah, love, let us be true
> To one another! for the world, which seems
> To lie before us like a land of dreams,
> So various, so beautiful, so new,
> Hath really neither joy, nor love, nor light,
> Nor certitude, nor peace, nor help for pain;
> And we are here as on a darkling plain
> Swept with confused alarms of struggle and flight,
> Where ignorant armies clash by night. (p. 402)

Post-Darwin and significant geological discoveries, so in the light of scepticism about the Bible's authority and the probable non-existence of God and heaven, Arnold suggests that nothing is certain, that life is a bleak struggle; positives ('true / To one another'), if found, are fragile and ultimately futile. Another letter from Conrad to Graham echoes this, as indeed does *Heart of Darkness*: 'The fate of a humanity condemned ultimately to perish from cold is not worth troubling about.[6] If you take it to heart it becomes an unendurable tragedy. If you believe in improvement you must weep, for the attained perfection must end in cold, darkness, silence. [. . .] Faith is a myth and beliefs shift like mists on the shore' (14 Jan. 1898; Conrad 1986, p. 17). *Heart of Darkness* states: 'Droll thing life is – that mysterious arrangement of merciless logic for a futile purpose' (p. 112).

John Davidson's 'Proem to *The Wonderful Mission of Earl Lavender*' (1899) captures the *fin de siècle* (end-of-the-century) sense of impending doom that many people (especially writers) felt at the time:

> Though our eyes turn ever waveward,
>   Where our sun is well-nigh set;
> Though our Century totters graveward,
>   We may laugh a little yet.
> [. . .]
> Though our thoughts turn ever Doomwards,
>   Though our sun is well-nigh set,
> Though our Century totters tombwards,
>   We may laugh a little yet. (p. 20)

Placing *Heart of Darkness* in its late nineteenth-century context will help you appreciate its darkness, its pervasive anxiety and sense of uncertainty, and provide a better understanding of Conrad's engagement with, for example, imperialism, the Other, and nature and nurture. But before you do any secondary reading, before you read any more of this study, I suggest you return to the novel and work out what you think.

NOTE ON THE EDITION USED

Quotations from *Heart of Darkness* throughout this study are from the Penguin Classics edition edited by Robert Hampson (2000). Hampson's introduction and notes are excellent, and the edition, which is relatively inexpensive and widely available, includes Conrad's *The Congo Diary*. Quotations are reprinted exactly. My ellipses are indicated thus: '[. . .]'.

CHAPTER 1

ON THE *NELLIE*

Works of fiction often contain in their openings hints and clues of what they are going to be about, seeds that are going to be developed.[1] James Joyce's 'Araby', for example, from his short story collection *Dubliners* (1914), opens with references to, among other things, blindness and sight, freedom, detachment, and consciousness. And the story is, in part, about blindness and sight, freedom, detachment, and consciousness. Mary Shelley's *Frankenstein* (1818) begins with several short letters from Walton to his sister that mention dreams and ambition, scientific discovery, creation and creativity, education, isolation and friendship. And the novel goes on to develop those references into key themes, among others. The opening of *Heart of Darkness* rewards detailed close reading and helps us to interpret and understand what follows, although with this dense and complex novel complete illumination is not possible. As Ted Billy says of the novel in *A Wilderness of Words: Closure and Disclosure in Conrad's Short Fiction*: 'every attempt at a definitive interpretation of the narrative ultimately falls short of a full disclosure' (p. 77). But perhaps that is what Conrad intended: the novel is in part about, as the following discussion suggests, the impossibility of 'definitive' interpretations, of texts, oneself, others and the world. Some things will always remain partially dark.

THE PRIMARY NARRATOR

The first 'character' we meet is *Nellie*, a 'cruising yawl' who 'swung to her anchor without a flutter of the sails, and was at rest'

(p. 15). We are told this, we discover shortly, by an unnamed narrator (also known as the 'primary narrator' or 'first narrator') who is on the boat with four other men: the 'Director of Companies' ('our captain and our host'), the 'Lawyer – the best of old fellows', the 'Accountant', and Marlow (pp. 15–16). Except that the narrator is not on the *Nellie*: he is recounting a scene from his past. We do not know why at this point, and later can only conjecture (in the same way that we can only conjecture why Marlow tells his story; discussed later in this chapter). We also do not know when the narrator is, presumably, writing. His text does not read like a spoken account. When he states, regarding the other men with him on the *Nellie*, 'Between us there was, as I have already said somewhere, the bond of the sea' (p. 15), he is referring to the opening of *Youth* ('Between the five of us there was the strong bond of the sea' (Conrad 1995, p. 9)),[2] the reference to a previously printed text linking the current text to the written/printed rather than the oral. Furthermore, the text is split (seemingly arbitrarily) into three numbered parts, which remind the reader of the authored materiality of the narrative.[3] These issues matter because they raise doubts concerning the reliability of what we read.

There are further problems for us with what the primary narrator writes. The opening, for example, is rather confusing:

The *Nellie*, a cruising yawl, swung to her anchor without a flutter of the sails, and was at rest. The flood had made, the wind was nearly calm, and being bound down the river, the only thing for it was to come to and wait for the turn of the tide.

The sea-reach of the Thames stretched before us like the beginning of an interminable waterway. In the offing the sea and the sky were welded together without a joint, and in the luminous space the tanned sails of the barges drifting up with the tide seemed to stand still in red clusters of canvas sharply peaked, with gleams of varnished sprits. A haze rested on the low shores that ran out to sea in vanishing flatness. The air was dark about Gravesend, and farther back still seemed condensed into a mournful gloom, brooding motionless over the biggest, and the greatest, town on earth. (p. 15)

The scene is difficult to imagine. Several terms – 'yawl', 'swung to', 'flood', 'made', 'offing', 'sprits' – rely on prior (nautical) knowledge and can hinder the imagining of the reader ignorant or uncertain of their meaning. It takes the whole passage (and possible re-reading) and, again, prior knowledge (or a map) to establish, approximately, where the *Nellie* is: on the Thames estuary between Gravesend and the sea, probably near Stanford le Hope, Essex.[4] The movement of the narrator's view can also be rather confusing: he looks approximately east to the nearby but extending 'sea-reach', then out to the 'offing' (the distant part of the visible sea), then nearer to the 'luminous space' in the middle-distance, then nearer still down to a 'haze' on the 'low shores' which are running 'out to sea in vanishing flatness', then approximately south-west to 'above Gravesend', then west, 'farther back still', to the air above London which seems (not actually is) 'condensed into a mournful gloom' that is 'brooding motionless'. The reader's eye has to continually adjust to the shifting and nebulous scene, and even slow re-reading gives only a semi-definite picture.[5] Why? The opening establishes that the novel is, in part, about 'indeterminacy' (Childs 2001, p. 80), about the inability to see clearly. But also about the ineffectuality of language, the inability of words to describe the world precisely, thus our inability to understand the world precisely (more is said below on these issues and in Chapters 3, on literary impressionism, and 4, on Kurtz's deathbed statement).

It is also possible that Conrad is exposing the narrator as untrustworthy, his narrative unreliable. The prose of the opening is overwrought and becomes rather repetitive. The 'mournful gloom, brooding motionless' above London, for example, becomes a 'brooding gloom' (p. 15), a 'gloom to the west, brooding' (p. 16), a 'gloom brooding' (p. 16) and a 'brooding gloom' (p. 18). The pathetic fallacy of, for example, 'brooding motionless' seems to suggest more about the narrator's mental landscape and prose style than it does about the phenomenal world: it is a curious conjunction fusing the unsettled internal with the static external.

F. R. Leavis, in his influential 1948 study of fiction, *The Great Tradition*, states:

There are [. . .] places in *Heart of Darkness* where we become aware of comment as an interposition, and worse, as an intrusion, at times an exasperating one. Hadn't [Conrad], we find ourselves asking, overworked 'inscrutable', 'inconceivable', 'unspeakable' and that kind of word already? – yet still they recur. Is anything added to the oppressive mysteriousness of the Congo by such sentences as:

It was the stillness of an implacable force brooding over an inscrutable intention [p. 60] – ?

[. . .] The effect of [the 'adjectival insistence'] is not to magnify but rather to muffle. (pp. 204, 205)

Writing after the influential Imagists (Ezra Pound, Ford Madox Ford,[6] H. D., Richard Aldington *et al.*), who at the start of the twentieth century had insisted on the clarity of the image and dismissed many Victorian authors for their verbiage,[7] Leavis blames Conrad for the repetition of certain adjectives and suggests that the muffling is a flaw. Chinua Achebe, in his controversial 'An Image of Africa: Racism in *Heart of Darkness*' (originally delivered as a lecture in 1975; first published in 1977), is even more critical:

The eagle-eyed English critic F. R. Leavis drew attention long ago to Conrad's 'adjectival insistence upon inexpressible and incomprehensible mystery'. That insistence must not be dismissed lightly, as many Conrad critics have tended to do, as a mere stylistic flaw; for it raises serious questions of artistic good faith. When a writer while pretending to record scenes, incidents and their impact is in reality engaged in inducing hypnotic stupor in his readers through a bombardment of emotive words and other forms of trickery, much more has to be at stake than stylistic felicity. Generally normal readers are well armed to detect and resist such underhand activity. But Conrad chose his subject well – one which was guaranteed not to put him in conflict with the psychological predisposition of his readers or raise the need for him to contend with their resistance. He chose the role of purveyor of comforting myths. (p. 3)

Where Leavis saw the repetition as a 'stylistic flaw' on Conrad's part, Achebe sees the repetition as 'trickery', an 'underhand activity' that induces 'hypnotic stupor'. Achebe goes further than Leavis because he believes that 'Conrad was a thoroughgoing racist' (p. 8). Achebe's essay is discussed in detail in Chapter 3; here, it is enough to note that both Achebe and Leavis do not take into account that the novel's lexis is, in the light of Conrad's other work, intentionally limited,[8] perhaps to suggest something about language and knowledge, but perhaps also because Conrad, 'undoubtedly one of the great stylists of modern fiction' (Achebe, p. 2), wants us to question the narrator and the reliability of what he writes.[9]

The examples of 'adjectival insistence' that Leavis and Achebe cite are from Marlow's narrative, yet the primary narrator is also adjectivally insistent, and both repeat 'brooding'. Given that two people's word stocks are individual and we each have our own voice (no one tells the same story in the same way), two fundamental questions arise: To what extent is Marlow's account exactly what he said, and to what extent has Marlow's story and story-telling technique influenced the primary narrator?

Frame narratives, or frame tales, are stories in stories: 'a classic framed tale would present a set of nested boxes, a set of brackets within brackets: an instance would be Mary Shelley's *Frankenstein*, where Walton's narrative encloses Frankenstein's narrative which encloses the Monster's narrative: when the Monster has finished his narrative, Frankenstein then finishes his, then Walton concludes' (Brooks, p. 351, n. 8). Frame narratives pose difficulties for the reader because they raise doubts about reliability; as Francis Mulhern says: 'authority is weakened, problems of interpretation deepen, and reading becomes less secure' (pp. 75–6).[10] How can Conrad's primary narrator remember everything Marlow said? He cannot. Even if he wrote up the story the day after being on the *Nellie*, and even if he had taken notes while Marlow was speaking, as Walton does with Frankenstein (pp. 17, 146), there would still be gaps in his records. What we read, then, is the primary narrator's version of events, and 'there is no formal guarantee that [what we are told] happened, or happened quite thus' (Mulhern, p. 76); 'the narrative frame filters everything that is said not just through Marlow but also through the anonymous narrator. At what point is it safe to assume that [. . .] Marlow expresses a single point of view?' (Brantlinger 1988, p. 257). This issue is important because it furthers the novel's interest in knowledge (what can we know for certain?), truth (how do we know for certain what is true and what is false?) and trust (can we trust anyone, even white middle-class men of the establishment?), but also in influence and understanding.

It is possible that Marlow's 'adjectival insistence' has influenced the narrator, making him repeat, for example, 'brooding', but it is also possible that the narrator makes Marlow adjectively insistent. And whether Marlow's story has been fully understood by the narrator is also uncertain. It is a question of judging tone and irony.[11]

How do we interpret, 'The air was dark about Gravesend, and farther back still seemed condensed into a mournful gloom, brooding motionless over the biggest, and the greatest, town on earth' (p. 15)? The 'seemed condensed into a mournful gloom, brooding motionless' and 'greatest' are problematic. The narrator supposedly looks towards London before Marlow speaks, so perhaps his view of the 'air' suggests something about his mood at the time and that he thinks that the capital city (and presumably what it stands for: empire, economic development, civilized values, morality) is a positive symbol. But the narrator is writing after Marlow's story and has perhaps been affected by it: perhaps he makes the air seem 'a mournful gloom, brooding motionless' to indicate something negative about the city and uses 'greatest' ironically.

The narrator goes on to say, regarding the Thames:

It had known and served all the men of whom the nation is proud, from Sir Francis Drake to Sir John Franklin, knights all, titled and untitled – the great knights-errant of the sea. It had borne all the ships whose names are like jewels flashing in the night of time, from the *Golden Hind* returning with her round flanks full of treasure, to be visited by the Queen's Highness and thus pass out of the gigantic tale, to the *Erebus* and *Terror*, bound on other conquests – and that never returned. It had known the ships and the men. They had sailed from Deptford, from Greenwich, from Erith – the adventurers and the settlers; kings' ships and the ships of men on 'Change; captains, admirals, the dark 'interlopers' of the Eastern trade, and the commissioned 'generals' of East India fleets. Hunters for gold or pursuers of fame, they all had gone out on that stream, bearing sword, and often the torch, messengers of the might within the land, bearers of a spark from the sacred fire. What greatness had not floated on the ebb of that river into the mystery of an unknown earth! . . . The dreams of men, the seed of commonwealths, the germs of empires. (p. 17)

There is, again, a problem of interpretation that raises questions about the narrator. Benita Parry, in *Conrad and Imperialism*, has observed: 'The opening address of the primary narrator, spoken in a voice that is alternatively bluff, ingratiating and oracular, can appear to be a portentous extolment of Britain's imperial might and the glory of colonial endeavours' (p. 24). Note, for example, the repetition of 'It had known', the personification of the river and the ships, the poetic, almost hyperbolic, language – 'knights all, titled and untitled – the great knights-errant of the sea'; 'the ships whose names are like jewels flashing in the night of time'; 'round flanks full'; 'gigantic tale'; and so on – and the rhetorician's climax: 'The dreams of men, the seed of commonwealths, the germs of empires.'

Parry goes on to argue:

Since each phrase of this ostensible tribute, in which recognition of mercenary motives is offset by praise for visionary impulses, is to be annulled by the fiction's action, these remarks necessarily serve as an object of irony, especially as the speaker with apparent innocence makes known that he and his companions, who are Marlow's audience, are all connected with 'overseas trade'. However, the imagist manner of his presentation, with its dualistic motifs, metonyms of menace and contrapuntal structure where every expression of positive sentiment is nullified by its opposite, is at odds with the conventions of celebratory rhetoric and makes the speaker an active communicator of irony whose very words carry the seeds of their own subversion. (p. 25)

To what extent, then, the narrator is in control of intended meaning is unclear, as is how much he has understood of 'the fiction's actions' contained in Marlow's narrative. Robert Hampson says that the passage begins with 'patriotic rhetoric [. . .] comfortingly familiar to the original readers of *Blackwood's Magazine*' (see 'Marlow's Audience', below, for details), but 'ends with more doubtful praise' (1992, p. 106). From 'Hunters for gold' to 'sacred fire': 'Every word is cunningly weighted: greed and pride are the implied motives for exploration; the sword (rather than the torch of religion and learning) is the dominant characteristic. And Marlow's first words – "this also . . . has been one of the dark places of the earth" [p. 18] – lead into a speech that continues this subliminal criticism' (p. 106). 'Hunters for gold and pursuers of fame' can indeed be interpreted as 'greed and pride' and 'the sword' certainly has more emphasis than 'the torch', but it is uncertain whether the primary narrator is being cunning. (Hampson's reference to *Blackwood's* might suggest he thinks that it is Conrad who is being cunning, which is possible, but also uncertain; the narrator's statement, 'as I have already said somewhere' (p. 15), which does not inspire confidence in him, reminds us that the narrator has written for *Blackwood's* and is perhaps doing so again.) If the narrator is being cunning, this would suggest that he is a subtle and self-conscious writer, which contradicts Parry's portrait of him and the possibility that the repetition of 'brooding' and 'gloom' is the product of a fallible writer.

Soon after the 'knights all, titled and untitled' passage (p. 17), Marlow comments: 'Light came out of this river since – you say Knights?' (p. 19). This reveals that a version of the passage was a speech made on the *Nellie*, presumably by the narrator. This means that it occurred before Marlow began his story, before the narrator could be affected (or not) by his meditation on empire and imperialism. If what we read is almost verbatim (it will not be completely) of what was said, it is likely that the passage is simply a 'portentous extolment of Britain's imperial might and the glory of colonial endeavours' (Parry, p. 24) that the narrator knows will soon be exposed by Marlow's story (if he has understood it). If he has understood Marlow's story, the narrator's willingness to be honest, to admit his ignorance about the ingloriousness of imperialism and 'colonial endeavours', is admirable, although why he does not present the speech as a speech raises doubts about his honesty and trustworthiness as a narrator. Once again, the reader is left questioning and suspicious of the narrator's character and his ability as a storyteller.

Regarding a later passage, during Marlow's narrative, where the primary narrator states, 'The others might have been asleep, but I was awake. I listened, I listened on the watch for the sentence, for the word, that would give me the clue to the faint uneasiness inspired by this narrative' (p. 50), Peter Brooks has observed that the narrator here 'characterizes himself as an obtuse [unperceptive, insensible, slow to understand] narratee, for pinning down "the sentence" and "the word" is precisely what Marlow's narrative will not and cannot do – indeed, what Marlow's narratives never do, according to the first narrator's own characterization of them as "inconclusive" [p. 21]' (p. 259). The primary narrator might, of course, be being knowingly self-deprecating, but he might be being unknowingly honest and be 'obtuse'.[12] There seems to be more evidence to support the latter, but nothing is certain, stable meaning is denied. And perhaps that is the point . . .

MARLOW

'Charlie' Marlow (pp. 23, 28) is 42 years old when he narrates *Youth*, which takes him back to when he was 'just twenty' (Conrad 1995, p. 10).[13] *Heart of Darkness* 'is narrated by an older and wearier Marlow who is haunted by the horrors he has witnessed in the Congo, and who realizes that the "dark places of the earth" [p. 18] include central London as well as central Africa' (Knowles and Moore, p. 220). The older Marlow has, as the primary narrator tells us, 'sunken cheeks, a yellow complexion, a straight back, an ascetic aspect', and who, sitting

15

'crossed-legged [. . .] with his arms dropped, the palms of his hands outwards, resembled an idol' (p. 16). He appears simultaneously fragile and poised, suggesting both fallibility and authority, and for readers is simultaneously troubling and assuring. This schizophrenia, or perhaps rather our schizophrenic response, is not resolved when Marlow speaks: we often do not know how to respond to him and are unsure of what he means.

The primary narrator warns us about this:

> The yarns of seamen have a direct simplicity, the whole meaning of which lies within the shell of a cracked nut. But Marlow was not typical (if his propensity to spin yarns be excepted), and to him the meaning of an episode was not inside like a kernel but outside, enveloping the tale which brought it out only as a glow brings out a haze, in the likeness of one of these misty halos that sometimes are made visible by the spectral illumination of moonshine. (p. 18)

As J. Hillis Miller says in his detailed reading of this passage, in '*Heart of Darkness* Revisited':

> Conrad's narrator distinguishes between two different ways in which a narrative may be related to its meaning. [. . .] The meanings of the stories of most seamen [. . .] are inside the narration like the kernel of a cracked nut. I take it the narrator means the meanings of such stories are easily expressed, detachable from the stories and open to paraphrase in other terms, as when one draws an obvious moral: 'Crime doesn't pay,' or 'Honesty is the best policy,' or 'The truth will out,' or 'Love conquers all.' The figure of the cracked nut suggests that the story itself, its characters and narrative details, are the inedible shell which must be removed and discarded so the meaning of the story may be assimilated. [. . .]
>
> It is far otherwise with Marlow's stories. Their meaning is outside, not in. It envelops the tale rather than being enveloped by it. (pp. 33–4)

And the 'meaning' brought 'out' is like 'a haze', like a 'misty halo': indeterminate, indefinite, evanescent.[14] As such, it presumably affects differently (if only subtly) each onlooker; it is observed and understood differently by each reader. As Conrad wrote in a letter of August 1897, 'one writes only half the book; the other half is with the reader' (Knowles and Moore, p. 124), and each reader will perceive and determine the 'haze' differently: 'one seeing more where the other sees less, one seeing black where the other sees white, one seeing big where the other sees small, one seeing coarse where the other sees fine. And so on, and so on' (James 1995b, p. 7). There are multiple readings, so multiple meanings; there is no single correct reading, so no central, stable truth. Nothing is certain; all is inconclusive.

The primary narrator seems to have a problem with this:

> it was only after a long silence, when he said, in a hesitating voice, 'I suppose you fellows remember I did once turn fresh-water sailor for a bit,' that we knew we were fated, before the ebb began to run, to hear about one of Marlow's inconclusive experiences.
>
> 'I don't want to bother you much with what happened to me personally,' he began, showing in this remark the weakness of many tellers of tales who seem so often unaware of what their audience would best like to hear. (p. 21)

This criticism sows doubts in the reader's mind as to the ability of Marlow as a storyteller, and in retrospect, having read his story, the reader is likely to agree with the narrator. It is, indeed, 'inconclusive', its 'meaning' nebulous. It also prompts similar questions asked of the primary narrator: How trustworthy is Marlow as a narrator? How reliable is his memory? To what extent did the events described happen thus?

Doubts about Marlow's reliability are often inspired by what he tells us. As Benita Parry notes, Marlow insists 'on his partial knowledge and imperfect understanding, his groping a way towards comprehending events into which he had been drawn' (p. 26); for example:

It was the farthest point of navigation and the culminating point of my experience. It seemed somehow to throw a kind of light on everything about me – and into my thoughts. It was sombre enough too – and pitiful – not extraordinary in any way – not very clear either. No, not very clear. And yet it seemed to throw a kind of light. (p. 21)

No, it is impossible; it is impossible to convey the life-sensation of any given epoch of one's existence, – that which makes its truth, its meaning – its subtle and penetrating essence. It is impossible. We live, as we dream – alone. . . . (p. 50)

'The tale Marlow tells becomes not only a version of, but an epistemological quest into, "the culminating point of my experience" [. . .]. The experience proves recalcitrant to Marlow's efforts to understand it. [. . .] Marlow's is the voice of a man desperately trying to create meaning' (Schwarz, pp. 63, 64).[15] But 'meaning' will be denied, or, rather, if created then it will be a comforting fiction, a rivet 'to stop the hole' (p. 51).

We also cannot trust the narrative of someone who admits to being confused: 'you lost your way on that river as you would in a desert, and butted all day long against shoals, trying to find the channel, till you thought yourself bewitched and cut off for ever from everything you had known once' (p. 59). Nor the narrative of someone who is uncertain: 'The steamer toiled along on the edge of a black and incomprehensible frenzy. The prehistoric man was cursing us, praying to us, welcoming us – who could tell? We were cut off from the comprehension of our surroundings' (p. 62). Nor the narrative of someone who was on the verge of a mental breakdown: 'I found myself back in the sepulchral city resenting the sight of people hurrying through the streets [. . .]. I had no particular desire to enlighten them, but I had some difficulty in restraining myself from laughing in their faces, so full of stupid importance. I daresay I was not very well at that time' (p. 114).[16] We should also be suspicious of a narrator who ends his narrative with a controversial lie (to the Intended; see Chapter 5), which echoes backwards through the story (the primary narrator's warning of Marlow's 'propensity to spin yarns' reverberates forwards), and whose story contains several other instances of lying: at the Central Station to the general manager's spy (p. 47), for example, and twice to Kurtz (pp. 106, 111).[17]

Furthermore, 'Marlow is repeatedly presented as a character whose personality is warped and whose vision is colored by subjective biases just like other of Conrad's characters, and as such Marlow's voice cannot be accepted unquestioningly by the reader' (Bonney, p. 154); this will be elaborated in the following chapters, but is relevant here in relation to Marlow on the *Nellie* and the possibility that he is 'warped' by his audience.

MARLOW'S AUDIENCE

Marlow tells his story to a 'Director of Companies', a 'Lawyer' (noted in *Youth* as being 'a fine crusted Tory, High Churchman' (Conrad 1995, p. 9)), an 'Accountant' (pp. 15–16) and their friend, the primary narrator, who is no doubt also bourgeois, establishment and religious (pp. 15–16). The frame narrative allowed Conrad to create Marlow's audience and he could have given him a tinker, tailor, soldier and spy. Instead, he chose a sample of the audience he knew would be reading the novel in *Blackwood's Magazine*: 'Conrad had a fairly clear conception of the nature of his immediate readership: conservative and imperialist in politics, and predominantly male (Hampson 2000, p. xxviii).[18] That readership would no doubt have been lulled into a 'false sense of security' by the primary narrator's 'nationalist history and imperialist rhetoric' (p. xxix) in his introduction. Marlow's narrative then questions the views and assumptions of his and Conrad's audience. Conrad thus draws in his readers, then slowly but surely challenges them.

One might ask why Conrad did not just expose the horrors of the Congo without such narrative tricks, why he did not confront his readers from the outset: such questions ignore the understandable dislike of being preached at. We are more likely to reflect on, and be affected by, rendered scenes and imaginative images rather than polemic. As Ford (1924) wrote, concerning what he and Conrad agreed the writer of fiction should and should not do: the author must never 'propagandise' (p. 208); he 'must learn to suppress himself: he must learn that the first thing he has to consider is his story and the last thing he has to consider is his story, and in between that he will consider his story' (p. 194).[19] It is also because the novel is about so much more than just imperialism.

In 'Listeners and Lies in "Heart of Darkness"', Thomas Dilworth discusses the 'active influence of listeners on speakers' (p. 110) and argues, among other interesting things, that Marlow, an untrustworthy narrator due to his lies, 'might not have praised "the idea" [of imperialism, in his prologue (p. 20)] or idealized the Intended if he had had an audience other than the Director of Companies, the Lawyer, the Accountant, and the primary narrator' (p. 521). 'If any audience can influence a speaker, this one can' (pp. 514–15). Marlow's narrative does, of course, expose European involvement in Africa, but it could have been more explicit, more shocking. Whether we blame Marlow for this, however, is problematic. Perhaps the primary narrator (or Conrad) altered Marlow's story because he knew he was writing for *Blackwood's*. We will never know for certain. What we do know for certain is that the primary narrator, Marlow and the other men on the *Nellie* pose problems for us as interpreters of the text, but also that we should embrace those problems, seeing them as part of the novel's engagement with late nineteenth-century 'uncertainty and doubt' (Watt 1980, p. 174), with questions about meaning, language, truth, and morality, issues that will be returned to in the following chapters.

CHAPTER 2

BEFORE THE CONGO

Minor characters can suffer for being titled thus, being easily over-
looked in favour of 'major' characters. But every character has a
role in a literary work, or presumably they would not exist; he or
she might not be fully worked out, might not be 'rounded', but their
life (or death) serves a purpose. Before Marlow gets to the Congo,
we hear about several 'minor' characters, each of whom foreground various issues and induce in the reader a sense of foreboding. Before we meet them, however, Marlow does some of the work.

MARLOW

On the *Nellie*, the world-weary Marlow, 'a haggard convalescent'
who tells a story 'conspicuously [lacking] the life-affirming *bon-
homie* of "Youth"' (Greaney, p. 65), gives us an insight into when
he was young, optimistic and ignorant:

> Now when I was a little chap I had a passion for maps. I would
> look for hours at South America, or Africa, or Australia, and
> lose myself in all the glories of exploration. At that time there
> were many blank spaces on the earth, and when I saw one that
> looked particularly inviting on the map (but they all look that)
> I would put my finger on it and say, When I grow up I will go
> there. (pp. 21–2)

The 'passion for maps' and daydreams of 'the glories of
exploration' are understandable: Marlow was an average

mid-nineteenth-century middle-class boy who probably also enjoyed Victorian adventure stories.[1] But as he grows up, he becomes, for the reader, rather troubling. He continues to look at one of the 'spaces', 'the biggest, the most blank, so to speak':

> True, by this time it was not a blank space any more. It had got filled since my boyhood with rivers and lakes and names. It had ceased to be a blank space of delightful mystery – a white patch for a boy to dream gloriously over. It had become a place of darkness. But there was in it one river especially, a mighty big river, that you could see on the map, resembling an immense snake uncoiled, with its head in the sea, its body at rest curving afar over a vast country, and its tail lost in the depths of the land. And as I looked at the map of it in a shop-window, it fascinated me as a snake would a bird – a silly little bird. (p. 22)[2]

The 'white patch' is no longer a 'blank space of delightful mystery'; it is now 'a place of darkness', a sinister phrase that inverts Marlow's description earlier of 'conquerors' tackling 'a darkness' (p. 20) and subverts the primary narrator's image of colonizers 'often' carrying a 'torch' (p. 17; see also Marlow as a supposed 'emissary of light' (p. 28)). Rather confusingly and ominously, Marlow still wishes to go there, but now because of a river that looks like 'an immense snake uncoiled'.

The passage is estranging because it is suffused with a sense of foreboding, and because Marlow is rather strange. He is a young man standing in central London looking at a map in a shop window and is like 'a silly little bird' 'fascinated' by a snake that is actually a river in 'a place of darkness'. The estrangement and foreboding continues when Marlow states:

> Then I remembered there was a big concern, a Company for trade on that river. Dash it all! I thought to myself, they can't trade without using some kind of craft on that lot of fresh water – steamboats! Why shouldn't I try to get charge of one. I went on along Fleet Street, but could not shake off the idea. The snake had charmed me. (p. 22)

The impetuosity – 'Dash it all!' – the scant knowledge – 'some kind of craft on that lot of fresh water – steamboats!' – the youthful bullishness – 'Why shouldn't I try to get charge of one' – and the charming of the 'snake' (which is, of course, full of biblical echoes): all comprise to make the reader suspect that Marlow, Eve-like, is going to suffer. Furthermore:

> I felt somehow I must get there by hook or by crook. So I worried them [his 'relations living on the Continent']. The men said 'My dear fellow,' and did nothing. Then – would you believe it? – I tried the women. I, Charlie Marlow, set the women to work – to get a job. Heavens! Well, you see, the notion drove me. (pp. 22–3)

The colloquial 'by hook or by crook' captures the spirited youthfulness of his aim, but it is undercut by: 'So I worried them.' Marlow means 'pestered them', but his language again carries negative connotations. As Peter Brooks has said: 'The desire for the journey is childish, absolute, persistent through contradictions; the journey itself appears compulsive, gratuitous, unmotivated' (p. 243).

Obsession and singleness of purpose in life and literature rarely result in a happy ending, and Conrad's readers are likely to have been reminded of the literary antecedents of Marlow's nautical compulsion. Robinson Crusoe, for example, notes that he:

> would be satisfied with nothing but going to sea, and my inclination to this led me so strongly against the will, nay, the commands of my father, and against all the entreaties and perswasions of my mother and other friends, that there seemed to be something fatal in that propension of nature tending directly to the life of misery which was to befall me. (1719; Defoe, p. 27)

Crusoe seems to defer responsibility for his 'propension', blaming it on a fatal flaw in his 'nature'. He thus might be implicitly blaming his parents while ostensibly praising them. The fatal flaw leads to a 'life of misery', but it also exalts him through its association with tragic heroes, the difference between them and him being that he lives to tell the tale. He is, therefore, doubly exalted.

The friendless, 'often depressed' (p. 15) Walton, in *Frankenstein* (1818), who is soon to be trapped on his boat, surrounded by polar ice, writes:

> This expedition has been the favourite dream of my early years. I have read with ardour the accounts of the various voyages which have been made in the prospect of arriving at the North Pacific Ocean through the seas surrounding the pole. [. . .] These volumes were my study day and night, and my familiarity with them increased that regret which I had felt, as a child, on learning that my father's dying injunction had forbidden my uncle to allow me to embark in a seafaring life. (Shelley, p. 14)

Walton's expedition is supposedly based on a philanthropic foundation – 'discovering a passage near the pole to those countries,[3] to reach which at present so many months are requisite', or 'ascertaining the secret of the magnet' (p. 14) – but his desire for success is complicated by 'failure' as a poet 'and how heavily I bore the disappointment' (p. 15).

Crusoe's and Walton's fathers command against their sons going to sea, and they were perhaps right to. Parents might sometimes know best. Marlow's aunt, however, does not: 'I am ready to do anything, anything for you. It is a glorious idea' (p. 23).

MARLOW'S AUNT AND FRESLEVEN

A 'glorious idea'?[4] This takes us back to the unconvincing assertion that what 'redeems' colonization 'is the idea only. An idea at the back of it; not a sentimental pretence but an idea; and an unselfish belief in the idea – something you can set up, and bow down before, and offer a sacrifice to. . . .' (p. 20).[5] The excessive repetition of 'idea' exposes its hollowness; it is reduced to an empty phrase. Marlow's taking charge of a steamboat will involve him, however indirectly, with the European 'conquest of the earth, which mostly means the taking it away from those who have a different complexion or slightly flatter noses than ourselves' (p. 20). His boyhood 'passion for maps' has mutated into something troubling.

Marlow's aunt is ignorant because, quite understandably, she believes what she reads and hears about the European involvement in Africa:

> I was also one of the Workers, with a capital – you know. Something like an emissary of light, something like a lower sort of apostle. There had been a lot of such rot let loose in print and talk just about that time, and the excellent woman, living right in the rush of all that humbug, got carried off her feet. She talked about 'weaning those horrible millions from their horrid ways,' till, upon my word, she made me quite uncomfortable. (p. 28)

Her use of 'weaning' is curious, given the masculine and violent foundation of colonialism. She is perhaps quoting some of the propaganda she has read. We are easily indoctrinated (and indoctrinate unquestioningly),[6] and as Chapter 1 of this study has discussed regarding the frame narrative, *Heart of Darkness* is in part about being suspicious of what people write and say. 'It's queer how out of touch with truth women are', Marlow states (p. 28). Is this misogynistic? Perhaps, if it is taken out of context: Marlow's story reveals that most people are 'out of touch with truth'.[7] The statement certainly exposes Marlow as ignorant and hypocritical: if women are distanced from 'truth', it is partly because of male-authored 'humbug' 'in print and talk', such as Marlow's lie to the Intended (see Chapter 5).

'Marlow's aunt asserts the idea of colonisation as a civilising mission', thus: 'In the early stages of the journey, the colonial theme is foregrounded' (Hampson 1992, p. 108). This foregrounding is reinforced by Marlow's anecdote about his predecessor, one of the Company's captains who 'had been killed in a scuffle with the natives' after 'a misunderstanding about some hens': 'Fresleven [. . .] thought himself wronged somehow in the bargain, so he went ashore and started to hammer the chief with a stick' (p. 23). The overreaction is bizarre; a man hammering someone 'with a stick' over a few chickens is comic. But the humour is, as humour often can be, problematic (we tend to laugh at, rather than with),[8] and our laughter is exposed as the anecdote continues, after another brief joke:

> Fresleven was the gentlest, quietest creature that ever walked on two legs [even more so than a hen]; but he had been a couple of years already out there engaged in the noble cause, you know, and he probably felt the need at last of asserting his self-respect in some way. Therefore he whacked the old nigger mercilessly, while a big crowd of his people watched him, thunderstruck (p. 23)

The 'stick' has become a club; the reader has become part of the crowd, shocked;[9] 'the noble cause' has been foregrounded and confused – the actions described are thoroughly ignoble – and in the light of the anecdote, Marlow's aunt's statement about 'weaning those horrible millions from their horrid ways' (p. 28) is brutally ignorant. Also foregrounded through Fresleven are the themes of insanity and absurdity, which Marlow will return to shortly and then throughout his narrative. Before he does so, he tells us that, by replacing Fresleven, he 'stepped into his shoes' (p. 24). The colloquialism is comic in its inappropriateness, but it is also loaded with foreboding as it sows the possibility in the reader's mind that Marlow's life on the Congo is not going to be the adventure he probably imagined it would be.

AT THE COMPANY'S OFFICES

When Marlow arrives in Brussels, he goes straight to see his employers and sign his contract. At the Company's office, he meets first a rather strange pair:

> Two women, one fat and the other slim, sat on straw-bottomed chairs, knitting black wool. The slim one got up and walked straight at me – still knitting with downcast eyes – and

only just as I began to think of getting out of her way, as you would for a somnambulist, stood still, and looked up. (pp. 24–5)

Often far away there I thought of these two, guarding the door of Darkness, knitting black wool as for a warm pall, one introducing, introducing continuously to the unknown, the other scrutinising the cheery and foolish faces with unconcerned old eyes. *Ave!* ['Hail!'] Old knitter of black wool. *Morituri te salutant.* ['Those about to die salute you.'] Not many of those she looked at ever saw her again – not half, by a long way. (p. 26)

Much has been made of these two passages and the old women in critical discussions of *Heart of Darkness*, and they are ideal for engaging here with some of the dangers when analysing characters and being influenced by critical material.

In the Penguin edition of the novel, used throughout this study, Robert Hampson's explanatory note for 'knitting black wool' states: 'the Fates of Greek legend, Clotho and Lachesis, who spin the thread of each man's life that is to be cut by Atropos' (Conrad 2000, pp. 130–1, n. 34). Hampson's gloss probably has its origins in Lillian Feder's 1955 essay, 'Marlow's Descent into Hell', in which she asserts, with great authority: 'In the company office, two women are knitting black wool. Conrad plainly uses these women to symbolize the fates, who, like Aeneas' guide, the Sibyl of Cumae, know the secrets of the heart of darkness' (p. 283).[10] A student studying the novel and relying on only Feder's essay or Hampson's note might, as Ian Watt writes humorously in his brilliant discussion of symbolism and *Heart of Darkness*:

ask such questions as: Why does Conrad give us only *two* fates? Which one is Clotho the spinner? and which Lachesis the weaver? Did the Greeks know knitting anyway? Where are the shears? What symbolic meaning can there be in the fact that the thin one lets people *in* to the room and then *out* again – a birth and death ritual, perhaps? (1980, p. 191)

The two women as two Fates is clearly reductive; the questions divert attention from the fact that 'a multiplicity of historical and literary associations pervades the scene in the anteroom; and this multiplicity surely combines to place the two knitters in a much more universal perspective. [. . .] It is not that the knitter reminds us [perhaps] of the classical Fates which really matters, but that she is herself a fate – a dehumanized death in life to herself and to others, and thus a prefiguring symbol of what the trading company does to its creatures' (Watt 1980, pp. 191, 192).[11] That 'prefiguring' is part of Conrad's use of characters in this section of the novel to foreground various themes and issues – colonialism, dehumanization, death, supporting unquestioningly a 'cause', indoctrination, and so on – and to instil foreboding in the reader.[12] It is best, then, to be careful of literary criticism, to ask whether it is being too reductive and narrow in its focus, ignoring contradictory evidence in the text being studied.

The themes of insanity and absurdity touched on with Fresleven are elaborated when Marlow eventually meets the Company's doctor:

'I always ask leave, in the interests of science, to measure the crania of those going out there,' he said. 'And when they come back too?' I asked. 'Oh, I never see them,' he remarked; 'and, moreover, the changes take place inside, you know.' He smiled, as if at some quiet joke. 'So you are going out there. Famous. Interesting, too.' He gave me a searching glance, and made another note. 'Ever any madness in your family?' he asked, in a matter-of-fact tone. I felt very annoyed. 'Is that question in the interests of science too?' 'It would be,' he said, without taking note of my irritation, 'interesting for science to watch the mental changes of individuals, on the spot, but . . .' 'Are you an alienist?' I interrupted. 'Every doctor should be – a little,' answered that original, imperturbably. 'I have a little theory which you Messieurs who go out there must help me prove. This is my share in the advantages my country shall reap from the possession of such a magnificent dependency. The mere wealth I leave to others. Pardon my questions, but you are the first Englishman coming under my observation . . .' (p. 27)

Even without knowledge of the historical context, it is clear that Conrad is writing at the expense of the doctor, who is rude – 'He smiled, as if at some quiet joke' – insensitive – 'Ever any madness in your family?' – and inhumane in his ambition: 'I have a little theory which you Messieurs who go out there must help me prove.' His method is also unscientific and rather ludicrous: he measures 'the crania of those going out' to Africa but not when they 'come back'. Whatever 'changes' have taken 'place inside', he can only guess at from what he hears; and Marlow's anecdote about Fresleven has already shown us that there will be gaps, uncertainty and personal interpretation in the reports the doctor might receive: Fresleven *'probably* felt the need at last of asserting his self-respect in some way' (p. 23; my emphasis). The doctor is interested in madness, but ironically does not seem to realize that, to appropriate Marlow's later comment about the French man-of-war, 'There was a touch of insanity in the proceeding' (p. 31).

William Greenslade, in *Degeneration, Culture and the Novel 1880–1940*, and John W. Griffith, in *Joseph Conrad and the Anthropological Dilemma*, have both written on Marlow's meeting with the doctor. Griffith writes, 'Conrad's doctor is a composite of many of the scientific interests of his day: craniology, incipient alienism, phrenology, and physical anthropology' (p. 160), which accords with Greenslade, who states: 'Satirising the contemporary fad for measuring skulls, as a means for establishing a client's propensity to deteriorate under stress, Conrad has Marlow suspect that the doctor is a fraud (a "harmless fool" [p. 27])' (p. 111). Greenslade's and Griffith's linking of the doctor to contemporary science, specifically craniology, is far more convincing than Feder's linking of the old women to the two Fates, partly because there is biographical material proving Conrad knew about, and scorned, many of the pseudo-sciences at the time,[13] partly because Conrad went on to satirize, in *The Secret Agent* (1907), some of the theories of Cesare Lombroso, the author of *Criminal Man* (1876) and *The Female Offender* (1895), which elaborate theories of phrenology, craniology, atavism, degeneration, and criminality,[14] and partly because other novelists at the time were engaging with similar subjects, notably, for example, Robert Louis Stevenson in *The Strange Case of Dr Jekyll and Mr Hyde* (1886) and Bram Stoker in *Dracula* (1897).[15] It is also possible that Greenslade and Griffith convince because, even though they are assured and assert a single reading – 'Conrad's doctor is a composite'; 'Satirising the contemporary fad for measuring skulls [. . .], Conrad' – their tone is more measured, more scholarly; Feder's 'plainly' – 'Conrad plainly uses these women to symbolize the fates' – is too assured, too assertive, and is, therefore, alienating.

After his dealings with his aunt and the Company's staff, Marlow feels like an alien: 'I don't know why – a queer feeling came to me that I was an impostor' (p. 29), a foreigner who is about to intrude on others. In the light of Marlow, his aunt, Fresleven and the Company's staff, the reader is likely to also feel uneasy. The 'snake' and the 'noble cause' await.

CHAPTER 3

ON THE CONGO

Marlow leaves for the Congo 'in a French steamer', the stopping of which 'in every blamed port' seems to be for 'the sole purpose of landing soldiers and customs officers':

> We pounded along, stopped, landed soldiers; went on, landed custom-house clerks to levy toll in what looked like a God-forsaken wilderness, with a tin shed and a flag-pole lost in it; landed more soldiers – to take care of the custom-house clerks, presumably. Some, I heard, got drowned in the surf; but whether they did or not, nobody seemed particularly to care. They were just flung out there, and on we went. (pp. 29–30)

In Brussels, responding to his aunt's talk of 'weaning those ignorant millions from their horrid ways', Marlow suggests 'that the Company was run for profit', to which she replies: 'You forget, dear Charlie, that the labourer is worthy of his hire' (p. 28), a biblical allusion to Luke 10:7, which Henry Morton Stanley cited also in his two-volume account of *The Congo and the Founding of Its Free State* (1885).[1] Christ states: 'And in the same house remain, eating and drinking such things as they give; for the labourer is worthy of his hire.' The aunt seems to use the allusion to propose that the Company's involvement in Africa is not one-sided (profit-driven), rather that there is a reciprocity between the Company and the Africans, that they both give and take in mutual agreement, for the benefit of both. Marlow's description of the seemingly endless landing of 'custom-house clerks to levy

toll' (to impose and collect duty on exports and imports) and soldiers 'to take care of the custom-house clerks' brings home to the
reader the scale of the European involvement and its dual foundation: money and violence. As Robert Hampson (1992) says:
'The French steamer introduces the machinery of repression and
exploitation' (p. 108). Marlow's 'queer feeling', in Brussels, that
he 'was an impostor' (p. 29), an alien about to intrude on others,
is confirmed by the image of the soldiers and clerks landing and
landing and landing, like a foreign invasion, and by Marlow
when he notes of the black men paddling a boat: 'They wanted
no excuse for being there' (p. 30). That some of the soldiers and
clerks probably 'got drowned in the surf' and 'whether they did
or not, nobody seemed particularly to care' also reveals the
devaluing of the lives of many European workers,[2] which was, of
course, hinted at by the blasé attitude of the plump controller in
Brussels, who 'had his grip on the handle-end of ever so many
millions' (p. 25). The aunt's statement that 'the labourer is worthy
of his hire' is, the more we read, increasingly ironic.

Continuing to describe travelling along the coast, Marlow also
mentions his 'isolation' even though he is surrounded by others
and of being kept 'away from the truth of things, within the toil
of a mournful and senseless delusion'. He says that the 'voice of
the surf heard now and then had a meaning' and that 'a boat
from the shore gave one a momentary contact with reality'; also
that looking at the black men paddling made him 'feel I belonged
still to a world of straightforward facts; but the feeling would
not last long' (p. 30). The 'truth of things', 'meaning', 'reality',
'facts': Marlow is touching on much that was suggested by
Conrad's use of the frame narrative and two unreliable narrators,
and by the primary narrator's description of Marlow's stories
(see Chapter 1). There is a sense that Marlow is slipping into a
solipsistic, epistemologically uncertain world, into 'the narrow
chamber' of his mind, 'of impressions unstable, flickering, inconsistent', where 'Every one of those impressions is the impression
of the individual in his isolation, each mind keeping as a solitary
prisoner its own dream of a world' (Pater, p. 235). And with that
slippage is an exposure of language as a tool to understand the
world and ourselves. As Ludwig Wittgenstein wrote, in 1921:

'*The limits of my language* mean the limits of my world' (p. 149). The specific meaning of the terms Marlow uses is unclear. What does he mean, for example, by 'reality'? It is a signifier (a sound-image) floating free from a clear signified (a concept).[3] Does he know what he means? The piling abstractions suggest not, suggest that he is clutching at words in the hope that something solid might be made from the epistemological haze.

The concern with language and meaning (or meaninglessness) continues with Marlow's description of the French 'man-of-war anchored off the coast' 'shelling the bush':

> Pop, would go one of the eight-inch guns; a small flame would dart and vanish, a little white smoke would disappear, a tiny projectile would give a feeble screech – and nothing happened. Nothing could happen. There was a touch of insanity in the proceeding, a sense of lugubrious drollery in the sight; and it was not dissipated by somebody on board assuring me earnestly there was a camp of natives – he called them enemies! – hidden out of sight somewhere. (pp. 30–1)

A 'touch of insanity' and a touch of absurdity: 'Absurd is that which is devoid of purpose' (Eugène Ionesco; Esslin, p. 23).[4] 'The shattering report becomes a "pop", the death-dealing shell a "tiny projectile"' (Berthoud, p. 46). Language exists to define, to pin down and explain, and it can, to a certain extent: eight inches is eight inches for someone who knows what an inch is. 'Pop' and 'tiny projectile' suggest that language might not always help us define and understand aspects of the world, especially when they are connected to human actions.

We are prompted to consider Marlow's language in this passage because he raises the issue of terminology: 'he called them enemies!' An enemy is an adversary, an opponent, a hostile force. A 'camp of natives [. . .] hidden out of sight somewhere' is not an enemy, in the same way that a man firing a gun into a forest does not have birds as his enemy, however much he hates them.[5]

The 'insanity' of the French man-of-war and the exclamation 'he called them enemies!' returns us again to Marlow's aunt's statement about 'weaning those ignorant millions from their horrid ways' (p. 28). In the light of what we have already witnessed, 'ignorant' and 'horrid' are terms that more appropriately apply, if generalizations are going to made, to the Europeans, not the Africans. The aunt's statement also prompts us to consider the meaning of the term 'civilised' and the relationship between language and point of view. More will be said about these issues when Marlow finally gets the Congo.

Between Brussels and the Congo, much has been confirmed and established for the reader about the Company, colonialism, money and violence, ignorance and knowledge, language and meaning and uncertainty. Also established is that a discussion of Marlow's journey should not be restricted to the Congo, that we should not be obsessed with the snake.

MARLOW, THE 'GROVE OF DEATH' AND THE ACCOUNTANT

Marlow finally gets to the Company's station, at Matadi (p. 32; p. 133, n. 56), 30 miles 'higher up' the Congo from 'the seat of government', Boma (p. 31; p. 133, n. 53), and from the boat he sees immediately a 'scene of inhabited devastation' (p. 32), but details are withheld until he has landed.

It is interesting that, upon landing, Conrad has Marlow encounter devastated objects before devastated people:

> I came upon a boiler wallowing in the grass, then found a path leading up the hill. It turned aside for the boulders, and also for an undersized railway-truck lying there on its back with its wheels in the air. One was off. The thing looked as dead as the dead carcass of some animal. I came upon more pieces of decaying machinery, a stack of rusty rails. To the left a clump of trees made a shady spot, where dark things seemed to stir feebly. (p. 32)

In *Cooking with Mud: The Idea of Mess in Nineteenth-Century Art and Fiction*, David Trotter writes: 'Rusty iron monsters, whether dumped on the slimy river-bank or ready for absorption into the furnace, became a potent emblem, in English literary tradition, of modern productivity, of modern wastefulness' (p. 166); 'For Marlow, the wreckage epitomises, almost as poignantly as the chain-gang which soon shuffles past, the wastefulness of empire' (p. 166, n. 10). The chain-gang comprises 'Six black men': 'Black rags were wound round their loins, and the short ends behind wagged to and fro like tails. I could see every rib, the joints of their limbs were like knots in a rope; each had an iron collar on his neck, and all were connected together with a chain whose bights swung between them, rhythmically clinking' (p. 33). The 'tails' of the men and the 'iron' of their collars link them to the animal-like railway-truck and the 'decaying' metal on the hillside. That link and the ordering of the scenes – devastated objects followed by devastated people – emphasizes the complete dehumanization of the men, the 'enemies', exposing that they are of equal, or lesser, worth as redundant machinery if they cannot be 'reclaimed' (tamed; civilized) for the 'great cause' (p. 33).

The juxtaposition of scenes is used again when Marlow walks into what he later names the 'grove of death' (p. 38):

Black shapes crouched, lay, sat between the trees, leaning against the trunks, clinging to the earth, half coming out, half effaced within the dim light, in all the attitudes of pain, abandonment, and despair. Another mine on the cliff went off, followed by a slight shudder of the soil under my feet. The work was going on. The work! And this was the place where some of the helpers had withdrawn to die.

They were dying slowly – it was very clear. They were not enemies, they were not criminals, they were nothing earthly now, – nothing but black shadows of disease and starvation, lying confusedly in the greenish gloom. Brought from all the recesses of the coast in all the legality of time contracts, lost in uncongenial surroundings, fed on unfamiliar food, they sickened, became inefficient, and were allowed to crawl away and rest. These moribund shapes were free as air – and nearly as thin. [. . .] The man seemed young – almost a boy – but you know with them it's hard to tell. I found nothing else to do but to offer him one of my good Swede's ship's biscuits I had in my pocket. The fingers closed slowly on it and held – there was

no other movement and no other glance. He had tied a bit of
white worsted round his neck – Why? Where did he get it? Was
it a badge – an ornament – a charm – a propitiatory act? Was
there any idea connected with it? It looked startling round his
neck, this bit of white thread from beyond the seas. (pp. 34–5)

This passage might seem to be, on first reading, easy to interpret.
Marlow sees a mass of black slaves dying; he notices one specifically, whom in a gesture of compassion he gives a biscuit and
around whose neck he sees a piece of white cloth, which he does
not understand; the purpose of the passage is to expose further
the inhumanity of the Europeans, except for Marlow, who is
empathetic. But more interpretative work needs to be done if the
text's complexity is to be revealed.[6]

The opening is difficult to imagine, rather confusing and rem-
iniscent of the indeterminacy of the novel's opening (see Chapter
1). 'Black shapes' obviously denies a clear picture, mainly
because of 'shapes' but also 'Black'. What does it actually mean?
Reading on, it becomes clear that the 'shapes' are black people
(how old? How many? Men and women?), but that does not help.
The term 'black' for skin colour is as unspecific and incorrect as
'white'. The 'Black shapes crouched, lay, sat between the trees,
leaning against the trunks, clinging to the earth'. The shift from
past tense – 'crouched, lay, sat' – to present – 'leaning', 'clinging'
– furthers subtly the sense of disorder and mutability, as does:
'clinging to the earth, half coming out, half effaced within the
dim light'; 'half coming out' creates two images, both of which
are nebulous. The people are 'half coming out' of the earth and
'half coming out' of 'the dim light'. '[A]ll the attitudes of pain,
abandonment, and despair' humanizes the 'shapes', to an extent,
but the 'attitudes' are still difficult to imagine, and we are not
helped because a mine explodes.

'They were not enemies, they were not criminals' is understandable as it refers back to 'he called them enemies!' (p. 31) and
the chain-gang: 'these men could by no stretch of the imagination be called enemies. They were called criminals' (p. 33). But
'they were nothing earthly now, – nothing but black shadows of
disease and starvation' is troubling. It is possible that 'earthly' is

another criticism of the colonists: the slaves are no longer useful, so they no longer have a purpose on earth. However, it is also possible that 'they were nothing earthly now' (they were no longer of the earth) is a supposedly compassionate description, which actually turns the people into an abstraction and in so doing dehumanizes them: the unearthly 'black shadows of disease and starvation' are denied a detailed elaboration of their very human suffering. Why there should be ambiguity is difficult to say. It is possible that Marlow does not have the language to describe the horror. The limits of his language have been set by past experiences and knowledge; the horror is something new, thus beyond his language. It is also possible that the clash of the literal – 'attitudes of pain, abandonment, and despair' – with the abstract – 'they were nothing earthly now' – reveals Marlow's confusion and, as Jesse Matz has suggested, is a way of trying to cope with the horror (p. 221).

Our problems as interpreters continue when Marlow looks down at a young man beside him: 'I found nothing else to do but to offer him one of my good Swede's ship's biscuits I had in my pocket.' The detail and clarity here is in stark contrast to the previous descriptions. A less detailed description would have been easier and easier to say – 'I found nothing else to do but to offer him a biscuit' – but it would perhaps have too strongly con-noted giving a pet a biscuit, although that connotation is still there in Marlow's statement. 'I found nothing else to do' implies that Marlow is at a loss, confused, helpless, but he seems to give the biscuit rather quickly. He could have got the man some water, which might have been a better (if still futile) action for someone who has been 'fed on unfamiliar food'. Marlow under-mines himself and, rather inappropriately at this point, no matter how 'good' he is, promotes the Swede. The statement and action are grimly, and presumably unintentionally on Marlow's part, comic and call into question the extent of Marlow's empathy.

Regarding Marlow's inability to understand the 'white worsted', Jesse Matz has written: 'The world of "straightforward facts" [p. 30] has vanished, replaced by one of obscure questions' (p. 221). Standing looking at the dying man, Marlow does not offer possible answers to those questions, perhaps understandably so, given the situation. That answers are not offered on the *Nellie* by the older, supposedly wiser Marlow is resonant. A possible interpretation of the 'white worsted' is that it symbolizes the strangulation, the murder, of Africans by those 'from beyond the seas'. Marlow's silence is perhaps because he really cannot interpret the worsted, which raises doubts about his wisdom. But perhaps the worsted is for Marlow something 'too dark altogether' (p. 123), something that he is unwilling or unable to speak about. He notes in passing that he 'was a part of the great cause of these high and just proceedings' (p. 33), but he also sets himself apart as an observer with a good line in irony. Perhaps the worsted shows that Marlow is an inextricable part, that he has blood on his hands. So too, then, do all the other white characters in the novel, including those on the *Nellie*, and many of those outside it: the imperialist readers of *Blackwood's*. Marlow's story is not a confession, a narrative for absolution, perhaps because 'innocent' and 'guilty' are too simple altogether. The divide between angels and devils is unclear, is perhaps an impossible distinction.[7]

Marlow meets an angel. Following his experience of the 'grove of death', he encounters the Company's chief accountant:

I didn't want any more loitering in the shade, and I made haste towards the station. When near the buildings I met a white man, in such an unexpected elegance of get-up that in the first moment I took him for some sort of vision. I saw a high starched collar, white cuffs, a light alpaca jacket, snowy trousers, a clear silk necktie, and varnished boots. No hat. Hair parted, brushed, oiled, under a green-lined parasol held in a big white hand. He was amazing, and had a penholder behind his ear. (p. 36)

It would be easy to think that Marlow's response to the angelic accountant is bizarre, but the juxtaposition of scenes must be remembered. Having witnessed horror in the grove, the 'unexpected', seemingly unreal accountant is an understandable relief. As T. S. Eliot writes in *Four Quartets*: 'human kind / Cannot bear very much reality' ('Burnt Norton', p. 178). What is problematic for us is Marlow's view once he has had time to gather himself, and his lack of qualification when on the *Nellie*:

> I respected the fellow. Yes; I respected his collars, his vast cuffs, his brushed hair. His appearance was certainly that of a hairdresser's dummy; but in the great demoralisation of the land he kept up his appearance. That's backbone. His starched collars and got-up shirt-fronts were achievements of character. (p. 36)

Given that Marlow knows the accountant supports the 'great demoralisation of the land', so is implicated in what he witnessed in the grove, his respect is troubling. It is unlikely that Marlow is being ironic[8] – 'His appearance was certainly that of a hairdresser's dummy' is the passage's qualifying statement, which suggests that the other statements are not being qualified, fully or partly, by irony.

Irony might be used later:

> I could not help asking him how he managed to sport such linen. He had just the faintest blush, and said modestly, 'I've been teaching one of the native women about the station. It was difficult. She had a distaste for the work.' Thus this man had verily accomplished something. And he was devoted to his books, which were in apple-pie order. (pp. 36–7)

The angel is not so angelic after all, and perhaps his 'faintest blush' is an acknowledgement of his impurity. Marlow's very English, very class-based, very pompous 'verily' and 'apple-pie order' strike one in their affectation as being the language of the accountant, whose expression 'to get a breath of fresh air' Marlow had noted as 'wonderfully odd' (p. 36). In a subtle act of ventriloquism, Marlow exposes the 'hairdresser's dummy', a performance reinforced several days later when the accountant exposes himself: 'When one has got to make correct entries, one comes to hate those savages – hate them to the death' (p. 38). It seems that Marlow is less judgemental of people when they are not directly exploiting the Africans: the Swede is a 'good' man; the accountant is fine until he admits to using one of the women.

As well as complicating our response to Marlow and problematizing various binary oppositions (innocent and guilty; angel and devil), the accountant is also important because 'it was from his lips' (p. 36) that Marlow first hears of Kurtz. But before he gets to him, Marlow experiences several other characters.

AT THE CENTRAL STATION

The main characters at the Central Station have two key functions in the novel: they make Marlow intrigued by Kurtz and they establish the idea of hollowness.

On arrival at the Central Station, Marlow does not care about Kurtz. When he meets the manager, who mentions that Kurtz 'was ill', Marlow thinks: 'Hang Kurtz' (p. 43). But he soon hears that Kurtz 'is an emissary of pity, and science, and progress', one of the 'gang of virtue' (p. 47), who had stated that 'Each station should be like a beacon on the road towards better things, a centre for trade of course, but also for humanising, improving, instructing' (p. 58). Taking into account the horror he has witnessed, his distaste for 'the philanthropic pretence of the whole concern' (p. 46) and the lack of 'moral purpose' (p. 55), and being 'surrounded by beings who are emotionally, morally, and spiritually void' (Watt 1980, p. 222), it is 'understandable that Marlow [. . .] should find himself drawn towards' Kurtz (Berthoud, p. 52).[9]

The emotional, moral and spiritual 'void' of the men at the Central Station impels Marlow to find an analogy, 'that of the hollow men':

> At the company station Marlow had seen the accountant as a hairdresser's dummy; here the brickmaker is a 'papier-maché Mephistopheles' who makes Marlow think 'that if I tried I could poke my forefinger through him, and would find nothing inside but a little loose dirt, maybe' [p. 48]; and the manager, who has risen to his position only because he is immune to disease, gloats that 'men who come out here should

have no entrails' [p. 42]. The hollowness of the manager is also spiritual. His smile suggests 'a door opening into a darkness he had in his keeping'; but Marlow suspects that the reason the manager never gave away 'the secret' of 'what could control such a man,' was that 'perhaps there was nothing within him.' [p. 42] (Watt 1980, pp. 222–3)

Their hollowness foregrounds Kurtz's – 'he was hollow at the core' (p. 95) – and helps Marlow to better understand him. But at the Central Station there is also the suggestion that we are all hollow.

To repair his steamer, which has been sunk, presumably, by the manager and his 'spy', the brickmaker who does not make bricks (p. 45),[10] Marlow needs rivets: 'What I really wanted was rivets, by heaven! Rivets. To get on with the work – to stop the hole' (p. 51). We are prompted to read this metaphorically when Marlow states: 'what I wanted was a certain quantity of rivets – and rivets were what really Mr Kurtz wanted, if he had only known it' (pp. 51–2). Rivets: things to help hide the existential hole of the self. Work, religion, 'Acquisitions' (p. 63), 'superstition', 'principles' (p. 71), family, hobbies: each can give one a sense of purpose, a centre for the self in an ever-changing, 'confused world'[11] and a bewildering universe. Each helps the individual ignore that life might just be a 'mysterious arrangement of merciless logic for a futile purpose' (p. 112).[12]

MARLOW, WHITES AND BLACKS

Another rivet might be a belief in otherness: a conception of the Other can give an individual, group or society a centre from which to see and judge, a sense of identity and superiority. As the feminist theorist Hélène Cixous says: 'Thought has always worked through opposition. [. . .] Through dual, hierarchical oppositions' (p. 101).[13] Man and Woman, for example, are constructed as an opposition but also as a hierarchy:

Man
Woman

The same can be said of European and African, and White and Black. Us and Them is a linguistic and ontological rivet that gives superiority and security to Us. However, (the) Master needs (the) Slave to exist: 'If you say that one thing is the opposite of another, you are at the same time asserting their mutual dependence, in that it is pointless to contrast two things from different categories' (Bennett and Royle, p. 209).

In their excellent chapter introducing reading racial difference in literary works, Andrew Bennett and Nicholas Royle consider Rochester's statement that contrasts Bertha Mason (a Creole from the West Indies) with the English Jane Eyre: 'look at the difference! Compare these clear eyes with the red balls yonder – this face with that mask – this form with that bulk' (Brontë, p. 322). Bennett and Royle note that:

> What is being asserted in Rochester's comparison [. . .] is not only difference but also likeness [. . .]. *Jane Eyre* [1847] articulates how racial otherness is constituted – both absolutely other, non-human, bestial, and at the same time an integral element in what defines racial sameness, in this case Englishness and, or as, whiteness. And it is this ambiguous status of the other (racial or otherwise) that makes it so threatening, so disturbing, so dangerous. (p. 209)

The Master would no doubt be troubled if he stopped to think that the Slave makes him Master and that the Slave is not literally Other. To reinforce the Master/Slave dichotomy and hierarchy, to strengthen the rivet, the Master probably also uses other negative terms: in Samuel Beckett's *Waiting for Godot* (1952), for example, the tyrannical yet vulnerable Pozzo repeatedly calls Lucky, his servant/slave, 'pig'. To reinforce the European/African, White/Black, Civilized/Uncivilized dichotomies, the white European might use 'enemy', 'criminal', 'savage' and 'nigger'.

By the time Marlow leaves the Central Station, he and the reader have encountered numerous whites – the aunt, for example, the doctor, the 'good' Swede, the accountant, the brickmaker – and numerous blacks – the paddling 'black fellows'

(p. 30), the chain-gang, those in the 'grove of death', the 'middle-aged negro, with a bullet-hole in the forehead' (p. 39), the 'beaten nigger' (p. 48). On the steamer to the Inner Station, there are several whites: the greedy, untrustworthy manager and 'three or four pilgrims' (p. 61; traders), one of whom is 'a little fat man, with sandy hair and red whiskers, who wore side-spring boots, and pink pyjamas tucked into his socks' (p. 68), and is a 'hopeless duffer' at steering the boat (p. 85). There are also several blacks: some cannibals, the poleman (p. 75), about whom we are told very little, the fireman and the helmsman.

Regarding the cannibals, Marlow says: 'We had enlisted some of these chaps on the way for a crew. Fine fellows – cannibals – in their place. They were men one could work with, and I am grateful to them' (p. 61). Later, when their leader, their 'headman' (Marlow's humour can at times be pretty weak), suggests to Marlow that they catch a native to 'Eat 'im', Marlow reflects: 'I would no doubt have been properly horrified, had it not occurred to me that he and his chaps must be very hungry. [. . .] They still belonged to the beginnings of time – had no inherited experience to teach them, as it were' (p. 69). Meditating on why the cannibals, wracked with hunger, did not eat him or the pilgrims, Marlow says: 'I looked at them as you would on any human being, with a curiosity of their impulses, motives, capacities, weaknesses' (p. 71). There are, then, interesting fluctuations and transitions in Marlow's discussion of the cannibals. He begins with an easy joke – 'Fine fellows – cannibals – in their place' – that would no doubt have got a laugh from the men on the *Nellie* (Chinua Achebe suggests 'in their place' is said by Conrad 'pointedly' (p. 5)), but Marlow immediately undercuts it with: 'They were men one could work with, and I am grateful to them.' The praise is, however, work-related, which might be seen as selfish, given Marlow's desire to get to Kurtz. That Marlow is not 'properly horrified' at them wanting to eat a native shows a degree of empathy that was perhaps lacking in the 'grove of death'. His acknowledgement that they had 'no inherited experience to teach them' not to eat human flesh is perhaps a judgement, implying that if they had been brought up as Europeans they would not be cannibals, but it seems to also acknowledge that they are who they are because of nurture, not nature, hence Marlow looking at them 'as you would on any human being': we are all essentially the same. Furthermore, the cannibals' 'restraint' (p. 71) contrasts with Kurtz's lack of restraint (p. 95) and that of many of the Europeans in the novel. In comparison to them, the cannibals are civilized. The hierarchical European/African, White/Black, Civilized/Uncivilized dichotomies seem to be weakening.[14]

The 'savage who was fireman' was:

> an improved specimen; he could fire up a vertical boiler. He was there below me, and, upon my word, to look at him was as edifying as seeing a dog in a parody of breeches and a feather hat, walking on his hind-legs. A few months of train-ing had done for that really fine chap. [. . .] He ought to have been clapping his hands and stamping his feet on the bank, instead of which he was hard at work, a thrall to strange witchcraft, full of improving knowledge. He was useful because he had been instructed; and what he knew was this – that should the water in that transparent thing dis-appear, the evil spirit inside the boiler would get angry through the greatness of his thirst, and take terrible ven-geance. (pp. 63–4)

Marlow's love of word-play, irony, litotes and hyperbole is rife, here. The man is not 'improved' because he can light and put water in a boiler; he is clearly not an 'edifying' sight because he has been made to do, not chosen to do, like a dressed-up pet; the 'training' has done little for him, except 'done for' him (put him in a situation that is impossible to escape: once 'civilized', there can be no complete return); and he is not 'full of improving knowledge', rather manipulative teaching. 'He ought to have been' left alone. Marlow does, however, find him 'useful', as he does the cannibals.

Regarding the passage, Chinua Achebe writes:

> As everybody knows [except for those who do not], Conrad is a romantic on the side. He might not exactly admire savages clapping their hands and stamping their feet but they have at

least the merit of being in their place, unlike this dog in a parody of breeches. For Conrad things being in their place is of the utmost importance. (p. 5)

It is unclear what Conrad does when not being 'a romantic on the side' (hating blacks who are not in their place?), or why Marlow's ironic simile, 'as edifying as seeing a dog in a parody of breeches', has become the denigrating, 'this dog in a parody of breeches'.[15] It is less unclear, but still troubling, why Achebe is talking about Conrad when it is Marlow speaking, and speaking through the untrustworthy primary narrator. Achebe thinks that Marlow is almost Conrad: 'Conrad seems to me to approve of Marlow, with only minor reservations – a fact reinforced by the similarities between their two careers' (p. 7). But in the light of all the questions raised by the frame narrative (see Chapter 1) and the presentation of Marlow, and of Conrad's life and other works,[16] it could also be argued that Conrad seems to disapprove of Marlow, with only minor reservations – a possibility reinforced by the differences between their two careers. We will never know for sure, but the novel and the use of biography certainly require a more nuanced approach than Achebe's. As Terry Collits has written: 'Achebe's "error" [. . .] was to misread *Heart of Darkness* as a stable embodiment of Conrad's political beliefs and attitude towards blacks. *Heart of Darkness* is a text too slippery to be pinned down in this way' (p. 98).

Achebe's approach to the novel is, broadly speaking, 'postcolonial'. Postcolonial literary criticism was inaugurated by Edward Said's *Orientalism* (1978), a critique of Eurocentric texts that assumed the superiority of the West and portrayed the Orient (the East) as its inferior Other. Postcolonial criticism thus draws attention to binaries such as West/Orient, White/Black, Europe/Africa – Achebe, for example, argues that Africa is set up 'as a foil to Europe' (p. 2) – but it often problematizes these binaries by stressing the hybridity of colonial/postcolonial cultures and the ambivalence of colonial/postcolonial discourses. Achebe's essay lacks much of this nuance and complexity, but it is nevertheless important as a robust challenge to Western hegemony at the time of its publication.[17]

Back to the steamer. The helmsman is an:

> athletic black belonging to some coast tribe, and educated by my
> poor predecessor [Fresleven] [. . .]. He sported a pair of brass
> earrings, wore a blue cloth wrapper from the waist to the ankles,
> and thought all the world of himself. He was the most unstable
> kind of fool I had ever seen. He steered with no end of a swagger
> while you were by; but if he lost sight of you, he became
> instantly the prey of an abject funk, and would let that cripple
> of a steamboat get the upper hand of him in a minute. (p. 75)

The helmsman does not just have earrings, he sports them, and
the long, blue 'wrapper' is presumably also on display. He
'thought all the world of himself': his vanity places him centre
stage as lead. But he is also the fool. His 'swagger' when Marlow
is near is a performance, but it hints at a truth: his anxiety when
on his own reveals insecurity, a fallible self behind the act. This
portrait of complex psychology stands in contrast to the presentation of many of the Europeans.

Marlow, once again, judges someone, but again it is on their
ability to work, not their race,[18] as he does the 'little fat' pilgrim
who is 'hopeless' at steering (p. 85). (Marlow seems to be troubled by weight and height: the old knitter in Brussels is 'fat' (p.
24) and the Company's head is plump and 'five feet six' (p. 25).)
When the helmsman gets killed, Marlow says:

> I missed him even while his body was still lying in the pilot-
> house. Perhaps you will think it strange this regret for a savage
> who was no more account than a grain of sand in a black
> Sahara. Well, don't you see, he had done something, he had
> steered; for months I had him at my back – a help – an instru-
> ment. It was a kind of partnership. He steered for me – I had
> to look after him, I had worried about his deficiencies, and
> thus a subtle bond had been created, of which I only became
> aware when it was suddenly broken. And the intimate profun-
> dity of that look he gave me when he received his hurt remains
> to this day in my memory – like a claim of distant kinship
> affirmed in a supreme moment. (pp. 84–5)

Marlow misses the man primarily because he now lacks a helmsman, however flawed, but also because there was a 'subtle bond' between them, as there is between the men on the *Nellie* (p. 15). Marlow's looking after and fussing over him also recalls the aunt's looking after and fussing over Marlow.

Regarding this passage, Achebe writes: 'It is important to note that Conrad, careful as ever with his words, is concerned not so much about "distant kinship" as about someone *laying a claim* on it. The black man lays a claim on the white man which is well-nigh intolerable' (p. 8). This is confusing. There is nothing in the passage to suggest that Marlow (or Conrad) finds the helmsman's look almost 'intolerable', a look which is '*like* a claim of distant kinship affirmed in a supreme moment', not *actually* the laying of a claim (an assertion of rights or ownership), nor *actually* a claim (an assertion). Furthermore, the scene is tender and humane, and stands in contrast to Marlow's response to the other deaths in the novel, including Kurtz's. 'And the intimate profundity of that look he gave me when he received his hurt remains to this day in my memory' is perhaps the novel's most powerful statement of compassion and regret.

Achebe also says: 'It is the laying of this claim which frightens and at the same time fascinates Conrad, "the thought of their humanity – like yours . . . Ugly"' (p. 8). He is here quoting from an earlier statement by Marlow; regarding the natives on the edge of the river, Marlow notes:

> No, they were not inhuman. Well, you know, that was the worst of it – this suspicion of their not being inhuman. It would come slowly to one. They howled, and leaped, and spun, and made horrid faces; but what thrilled you was just the thought of their humanity – like yours – the thought of your remote kinship with this wild and passionate uproar. Ugly. Yes, it was ugly enough; but if you were man enough you would admit to yourself that there was in you just the faintest trace of a response to the terrible frankness of that noise, a dim suspicion of there being a meaning in it which you – you so remote from the night of first ages – could comprehend. (pp. 62–3)

This is an audacious and challenging speech to make to the men on the *Nellie*, and to the readers of *Blackwood's Magazine*, and is clever rhetoric: acknowledging 'remote kinship' is unpleasant (the speaker is on the side of his audience), but denying the possibility of that kinship means you are a coward (the speaker challenges his male audience's masculinity and puts them in a position of no comeback; 'if you were man enough' is a rhetorical trump card). The passage reveals that the 'dual, hierarchical oppositions' (Cixous, p. 101) of European/African, White/Black, Us/Them are man-made constructs, linguistic and ontological rivets.[19] 'Racism is, before anything else, the delusion of essentialism' (Bennett and Royle, p. 210): the delusion that categories of people, such as Europeans and Africans or Whites and Blacks, have intrinsically different natures.

Just over half-way through his essay, Achebe states: 'The point of my observations should be quite clear by now, namely that Conrad was a thoroughgoing racist' (p. 8). The point of my observations should also be quite clear by now, namely that *Heart of Darkness* is too complex a novel for such a simplistic assertion. Marlow (not Conrad) certainly has a complicated and at times troubling relationship with blacks, but so too does he with whites. He uses the terms 'savage' and 'nigger', but he also challenges his listeners' assumptions about 'savages' and 'niggers'. If splitting people into White and Black is ignorant and unproductive, and perpetuates denigrating categorization, then so too is splitting them into Racist and Unracist.

But perhaps my interpretation of the novel is skewed by my relationship with Conrad, who I do not like to think was racist, and by my ethnic and cultural make up. New Historicism and cultural materialism, two 'schools' of literary theory and criticism that emerged in America and Britain respectively in the 1980s, argue that the act of interpreting the past is never impersonal, objective or ahistorical; it is always personal, subjective and of its time.[20] 'We bring ourselves and our conflicts to words, to poems and pictures [. . .]; and thus we change the poems and the pictures' (Kermode, p. 432). But this is not cause for concern, so long as critics and students are aware that they and others might be manipulating texts for their own (perhaps polemical, perhaps selfish) ends.

CHAPTER 4

AT THE INNER STATION

Approximately 'a mile and a half below Kurtz's station' (p. 74), an important event happens that throws some light on several fundamental ideas underpinning the novel. It can also inform an understanding of Kurtz.

Navigating a particularly difficult channel, Marlow:

> was looking down at the sounding-pole, and feeling much annoyed to see at each try a little more of it stick out of that river, when I saw my poleman give up the business suddenly, and stretch himself flat on the deck, without even taking the trouble to haul his pole in. He kept hold on it though, and it trailed in the water. At the same time the fireman, whom I could also see below me, sat down abruptly before his furnace and ducked his head. I was amazed. Then I had to look at the river mighty quick, because there was a snag in the fairway. Sticks, little sticks, were flying about – thick: they were whizzing before my nose, dropping below me, striking behind me against my pilot-house. All this time the river, the shore, the woods, were very quiet – perfectly quiet. I could only hear the heavy splashing thump of the stern-wheel and the patter of these things. Arrows, by Jove! We were being shot at! I stepped in quickly to close the shutter on the landside. (p. 75)

The reader is, here, on the boat with Marlow and experiencing events as he experiences them: when Marlow sees the poleman lie down and then the fireman sit down, but does not know why, the reader also sees them but also does not know why. When Marlow looks back at the river and then sees 'little sticks [. . .] flying about', so too does the reader. When Marlow realizes that the sticks are 'Arrows, by Jove!' and that the boat is 'being shot at', the reader also realizes.

In *Conrad in the Nineteenth Century*, Ian Watt named and defined 'delayed decoding' (p. 175). 'Conrad's device of delayed decoding represents an original narrative solution to the general problem of expressing the process whereby the individual's sensations of the external world are registered and translated into the causal and conceptual terms which can make them understandable to the observer and communicable to other people' (p. 179). Delayed decoding 'takes us directly into the observer's consciousness at the very moment of the perception, before it has been translated into its cause' to show 'the gap between impression and understanding; the delay in bridging the gap enacts the disjunction between the event and the observer's trailing understanding of it' (pp. 175, 176–7).

In the scene quoted above, for example, there is an obvious delay in Marlow's (and the reader's) understanding of what is going on. 'Sticks, little sticks' is his first impression of whatever is 'flying about'; he then, after a delay, realizes that they are arrows, which is followed by the realization of the cause: the boat is 'being shot at'. Once this cognitive process has taken place, he can then also understand the poleman lying down and the fireman sitting.[1]

As the barrage from the forest continues, so too does the use of delayed decoding:

Something big appeared in the air before the shutter, the rifle went overboard, and the [helmsman] stepped back swiftly, looked at me in an extraordinary, profound, familiar manner, and fell upon my feet. The side of his head hit the wheel twice, and the end of what appeared a long cane clattered round and knocked over a little camp-stool. It looked as though after wrenching that thing from somebody ashore he had lost his balance in the effort. The thin smoke had blown away, we were clear of the snag, and looking ahead I could see that in another hundred yards or so I would be free to sheer off, away from the bank; but my feet felt so very warm and wet that I had to look down. The man had rolled on his back and stared straight up at me; both his hands clutched that cane. It was the shaft of a spear that, either thrown or lunged through the opening, had caught him in the side just below the ribs; the blade had gone in out of sight, after making a frightful gash; my shoes were full; a pool of blood lay very still, gleaming dark-red under the wheel; his eyes shone with an amazing lustre. (p. 77)

'Sticks' to 'Arrows' is a two-stage process, as is 'my feet felt so very warm and wet' to 'my shoes were full'. But as Cedric Watts has noted (1984, p. 44), the scene also contains a three-stage process: the helmsman falls over for no apparent reason – the helmsman falls over 'after wrenching [a cane] from somebody ashore' – the helmsman falls over because of a spear. Similarly, 'Something big' becomes a 'long cane', which becomes 'a spear'.[2]

Ian Watt relates Conrad's use of delayed decoding to Impressionist painting, late nineteenth-century 'epistemological solipsism' (1980, p. 172) and literary impressionism, arguing that *Heart of Darkness* is 'impressionist' because 'it accepts, and indeed in its very form asserts, the bounded and ambiguous nature of *individual* understanding' (p. 174; my emphasis). As John G. Peters has written: 'For impressionism [and the literary impressionist], all experience is individual, and every experience of objects of consciousness is unique' (p. 20).[3] To clarify what Watt and Peters are saying, it is best to return to the novel.

From the forest, arrows are being shot at the boat. Upon realizing what they are, the poleman lies down but continues to hold the pole, the fireman sits down and ducks his head, and Marlow closes the shutter. One event is responded to in three different ways. Furthermore, Marlow first sees 'sticks' then realizes that they are arrows. It is possible that the poleman saw arrows immediately (and was reminded of his mother, who was killed by an arrow), the helmsman saw poisoned darts (and noticed on the floor of the steamer a mosquito, then thought about poisoned darts and proboscis). Three people, three consciousnesses, three points of view. If there were 20 other people experiencing the event, there would have been 20 other points of view, 20 other responses. As Henry James says, we are 'each watching the same show, but one seeing more where the other sees less, one seeing black where the other sees white, one seeing big where the other sees small, one seeing coarse where the other sees fine. And so on, and so on' (James 1995b, p. 7).[4] The external world is unstable: there is not a common phenomenal world which passes unfiltered into everyone's brains.[5] The world is different according to each individual consciousness, hence: 'every experience of objects of consciousness is unique'. And the world is different each day for each consciousness because 'the individual is a succession of individuals' (Beckett 1999, p. 19); every day alters us, so every day is experienced by a different 'I'. What things 'mean' are thus also different for each person. An arrow in the air for someone might 'mean' an act of aggression, for another an act of defence. And if everything is so open, so hazy, so uncertain regarding the external world, the internal world must also be as open, as hazy, as uncertain. In his 'Preface to *The Nigger of the "Narcissus"'* (1897), Conrad stated: 'My task which I am trying to achieve is, by the power of the written word, to make you hear, to make you feel – it is, before all, to make you *see!*' (1979, p. 147). Delayed decoding makes us see how we see and think about how we think. It reminds us that we each have our own sense of the world and our own meanings that we cling on to to stop us falling into an 'abyss of Chaos',[6] an existential darkness where nothing is certain. Where does 'meaning' and 'truth' lie? Perhaps impressions, being unmediated by reason, tell us something more fundamental about ourselves and our view of and relationship with the world.[7] John Dowell, the narrator of Ford Madox Ford's *The Good Soldier* (1915), asks: 'If for nine years I have possessed a goodly apple that is rotten at the core and discover its rottenness only in nine years and six months less four days, isn't it true to say that for nine years I possessed a goodly apple?' (p. 12). The rotten apple was a goodly apple for Dowell because he believed it to be a goodly apple. Every impression we have, and decoded impression, and every view and every belief, might turn out to be rotten apples. But they might not be.

Conrad also invites us to consider that the knowledge we have will always be incomplete: we can realize that a cane, for example, is a spear, but was it 'thrown or lunged'?[8] Answers prompt questions prompt answers prompt questions – leaving not light or enlightenment, but the dark of solipsism. We can never fully understand. The 'most you can hope [for] is some knowledge of yourself' (p. 113), and that might not be a good thing.

Soon after the attack on the steamer, we arrive at the Inner Station. By now we have heard that Kurtz is 'a very remarkable person' (p. 37), 'an exceptional man' (p. 43), 'an emissary of pity, and science, and progress' (p. 47), a 'universal genius' (p. 51), 'a gifted creature' (p. 79), but also someone who needed 'rivets [. . .] if only he had known it' (pp. 51–2), whose fiancée was 'out of it' (p. 80), who had been 'claimed' by 'powers of darkness', 'had taken a high seat amongst the devils of the land' (p. 81), was an 'initiated wraith' (p. 82), and had presided over 'certain midnight dances ending with unspeakable rites' (p. 83);[9] who was also a painter of a 'sinister' sketch (pp. 46–7),[10] 'little more than a voice' (p. 80) and an eloquent author of 'noble words' who had 'scrawled' at the end of his report for the 'International Society for the Suppression of Savage Customs', 'Exterminate all the brutes!' (pp. 83–4).[11] Our impression of Kurtz is, then, like an Impressionist painting: hazy, indistinct, open to interpretation. And the impressionistic attack scene, with its use of delayed decoding, is a warning that we may never have a clear picture of who Kurtz is and what he means. Understanding may be delayed indefinitely.

WHAT IS KURTZ?

At the Central Station, overhearing the manager and his uncle chat conspiratorially, Marlow learns that Kurtz once wrote: 'Each station should be like a beacon on the road towards better things, a centre for trade of course, but also for humanising, improving, instructing' (p. 58). At the Inner Station, Marlow hears from the Russian about what seems to be a radically different Kurtz.[12] Regarding Kurtz's expeditions for ivory, Marlow quickly realizes that Kurtz was not trading goods for ivory. Using guns and cartridges, 'he raided the country' (p. 92). Furthermore, he 'got the tribe to follow him': 'he came to them with thunder and lightning, you know – and they had never seen anything like it – and very terrible.[13] He could be very terrible. You can't judge Mr Kurtz as you would an ordinary man' (p. 92). The Russian seems to be implying here that Kurtz is god-like, so is outside common categories of judgement, of 'right' and 'wrong', but his following story leads Marlow to a type of judgement. The Russian tells Marlow how Kurtz 'declared he would shoot me unless I gave him the ivory and then cleared out of the country, because he could do so, and had a fancy for it, and there was nothing on earth to prevent him killing whom he jolly well pleased' (p. 92), then about Kurtz disappearing 'for weeks' to 'forget himself', to which Marlow declares: 'Why! he's mad' (p. 93). This is a lazy conclusion that deals easily with Kurtz. It makes him Other, relying as it does on the socially constructed dichotomy of Sane/Insane.[14]

Later, however, having spoken with Kurtz, Marlow says that he 'wasn't arguing with a lunatic [. . .]. Believe me or not, his intelligence was perfectly clear – concentrated, it is true, upon himself with horrible intensity, yet clear [. . .]. But his soul was mad. Being alone in the wilderness, it had looked within itself, and, by heavens! I tell you, it had gone mad' (p. 107). Marlow thus shifts the issue of madness from mind to 'soul', but what he means by 'soul' is unclear. He later refers to 'the inconceivable mystery of a soul that knew no restraint, no faith, and no fear, yet struggling blindly with itself' (p. 108), and asserts that Kurtz 'had pronounced a judgment upon the adventures of his soul on this earth' (p. 112). In the light of these comments and Kurtz being, according to Marlow, 'hollow at the core' (p. 95), which recalls the emotional, moral and spiritual void of the men at the Central Station (see Chapter 3), and his view that life is a 'mysterious arrangement of merciless logic for a futile purpose' (p. 112), it seems that by 'soul' Marlow does not to mean a spiritual (religious) part of the self that is distinct from the body. It is more likely that the personified 'soul' is the 'principle' (foundation; basis) of the self: the base of being, unsocialized, untouched by the 'nets' of 'nationality, language, religion', free of man-made dichotomies.[15]

Reflecting on the 'heads on the stakes' (p. 94), Marlow says: 'They only showed that Mr Kurtz lacked restraint in the gratification of his various lusts, that there was something wanting in him – some small matter which, when the pressing need arose, could not be found under his magnificent eloquence' (p. 95). What Kurtz's 'various lusts' were, Marlow does not clarify, and as Jacques Berthoud has said: 'Some critics have complained that Conrad has been insufficiently specific about the inconceivable ceremonies [p. 95; the "midnight dances ending with unspeakable rites" (p. 83)] and nameless lusts' (p. 54). But perhaps the insufficient specificity is understandable. It could be that Marlow just does not know: he shouts at the Russian that he does not 'want to know anything of the ceremonies used when approaching Kurtz' (p. 95) and he only 'reluctantly gathered from what I heard at various times' about rites being 'offered up to' Kurtz (p. 83), which suggests lack of detail.

Andrew Michael Roberts offers another view:

> What were [the] 'unspeakable rites', bearing in mind that they involved 'various lusts' [actually, the two are not necessarily connected] and that Marlow apparently cannot bring himself to be specific about them? [. . .] The conclusion, I think, has to be that what Kurtz has done is precisely the non-specified or unspeakable: it is less any set of actual actions than a symbolic location of taboo-breaking. As such, and in the historical context of the turn of the century, it can hardly fail to evoke the homophobic taboo of 'the love that dare not speak its name'.[16] Perhaps the closest that Marlow comes to identifying the unspeakable is when he finds it intolerable to hear about 'the ceremonies used when approaching Mr. Kurtz' [p. 95], which seem to involve crawling. (p. 133)

If I am reading this correctly, and in the light of Roberts's suggestion that 'an interpretation of "Heart of Darkness" in terms of male homosexual desire can undoubtedly be made' (p. 131), Roberts seems to be implying that Kurtz sodomized some of the natives, or watched some of the natives sodomize each other. It is possible. Whether Marlow's 'Ah, he talked to you of love!' and

the Russian's cry, 'It isn't what you think' (p. 91), confirm or con-
tradict this interpretation is open to speculation.

Regarding Marlow's silence, Michael Greaney has suggested:
'Perhaps Marlow realizes that some things are best left to the
imagination, that his listeners, noticing those tell-tale gaps and
consciously lame euphemisms, are free to interpolate whatever
imaginary abominations gratify their own prurience' (p. 73).
'What is thinkable is also possible' (Wittgenstein, p. 43).
However, those who write about the novel are not so free as they
must support their interpretations with quotations. Roberts, with
justification, seems to insert into the gap Kurtz's sexuality; with
justification, you can insert other things.[17]

Marlow later comments: 'I tried to break the spell – the heavy,
mute spell of the wilderness – that seemed to draw him to its piti-
less breast by the awakening of forgotten and brutal instincts, by
the memory of gratified and monstrous passions. This alone, I
was convinced, had driven him out to the edge of the forest, to
the bush, towards the gleam of fires, the throb of drums, the
drone of weird incantations; this alone had beguiled his unlaw-
ful soul beyond the bounds of permitted aspirations' (p. 107).
The use of 'aspirations' reminds us of Kurtz's early ambitions
that were mocked by the manager and his uncle: 'Each station
should be like a beacon on the road towards better things, a
centre for trade of course, but also for humanising, improving,
instructing' (p. 58); 'permitted' reminds us that there are, from a
European perspective here, written and unwritten codes of
ethical conduct. Kurtz and the 'pilgrims', for example, have lost
sight of those codes, but as Robert Hampson observes: 'there
remain essential differences between Kurtz and the "pilgrims".
He is a man of good intentions who has betrayed his ideals
through the will-to-power that was implicit in them' (1992,
p. 111). 'Will-to-power' is a term derived from the influential
nineteenth-century German philosopher Friedrich Nietzsche.
Nietzsche presented 'will to power' as 'a principle discernible in
all nature, in accordance with which a self or "centre of power"
[a group or society, for instance] expands beyond its own boundaries, asserts itself over another and strives to appropriate it'
(Stern, p. 80). Belgian and British colonialism, for example, are

acts of will to power: to put it simply, Europeans enter another country, assert themselves over the natives and attempt to own them and their landscape. Hampson is suggesting that Kurtz's 'ideals' of 'humanising, improving, instructing' contain will to power: they are inherently Us (human/humane – civilized) and Other (bestial, in need of improving and instructing – uncivilized). (His report for the 'International Society for the Suppression of Savage Customs' states: 'By the simple exercise of our will we can exert a power for good practically unbounded' (p. 83).) Kurtz's judgements are thus based on dangerous dichotomies, which surely raise questions about him being 'a man of good intentions'.[18] In his defence, Kurtz could, of course, acknowledge his ignorance – and perhaps he does at the end. The will to power in his ideals also complicates the divide between the 'original' Kurtz and the Kurtz who 'lacked restraint in the gratification of his various lusts'. Perhaps the desire to humanize, improve and instruct is as problematic as the heads on stakes. Kurtz has not become Other, rather 'a ghastly parody of civilization' (Berthoud, p. 57).

Marlow informs his listeners that the 'original Kurtz had been educated partly in England [. . .]. His mother was half-English, his father half-French. All Europe contributed to the making of Kurtz' (pp. 82–3). Regarding Kurtz's 'lusts', we should remind ourselves of the difference between the starving cannibals and Kurtz. Marlow assumed that extreme hunger (something of the body) would over-power 'superstition, beliefs, [. . .] principles' (things of the mind); he suggests that it would surely be 'easier to face bereavement, dishonour, and the perdition of one's soul' than to fight 'prolonged hunger' (p. 71). The cannibals, however, have 'restraint', even though 'They still belonged to the beginnings of time – had no inherited experience to teach them, as it were' (p. 69). Kurtz, constructed by modern Europe, socialized by 'inherited experience', 'lacked restraint' (p. 95). 'Europe must', then, 'bear some of the blame for his downfall' (Greaney, p. 73). But not all of the blame; that would be too easy: to defer individual responsibility is, as Edmund says in *King Lear*, 'the excellent foppery of the world [. . .]. An admirable evasion of whoremaster man' (1.2.118, 126–7). Kurtz, painter, poet, musician, journalist, potential politician, 'universal genius' (p. 116), the 'representative of civilized Western Europe', went 'wrong', suggesting that if he can do so, then so can anybody (Simmons, p. 88): Marlow, the novel's true Everyman, hungry, begins to get 'savage' (p. 43);[19] there is the potential in us all to lack restraint, to go 'wrong'. The cannibals, restrained, actually civilized, show us the other side of our potential.

Kurtz dies whispering: 'The horror! The horror!' (p. 112). The possible meaning of his last four words has generated many, many more, so many that the whisper is, like the 'unspeakable rites' and unknown lusts, clearly a gap in the text that will never be filled with one definitive interpretation.[20] But perhaps that is the point. There is no such thing as a definitive interpretation, of novels, oneself, others, or life. There are only points of view.

What is Kurtz? He is 'an impenetrable darkness' (p. 111), but he also sheds some light; he is an anti-climax, but also a climax of many of the novel's concerns: colonialism, imperialism, race, essence and existence, nature and nurture, belief systems, dichotomies, sanity and madness, power, greed, violence, restraint, certainty and uncertainty. He is 'just a word' (p. 50), but as a dreaming yet fallible being, he is also very human.

Heart of Darkness is not 'about' the 'break-up of one petty European mind' (Achebe, p. 8). It is about past selves and present selves, and a warning about possible future selves, irrespective of race, creed or colour. Whether it is optimistic or pessimistic, that is for you to decide.

CHAPTER 5

KURTZ'S WOMEN?

The African woman: black and savage; Marlow has a problem with her, but at least she is in her place. The European Intended: white and refined; Marlow does not have a problem with her, and she is in her place. The presentation of the two main women characters reinforces the hierarchical dichotomies of Man/Woman, White/Black, and Civilized/Bestial.

If only things were so simple.

THE 'WILD AND GORGEOUS' AFRICAN WOMAN

Soon after arriving at the Inner Station, following a conversation with the Russian and a brief meeting with Kurtz, Marlow sees the African woman:

[F]rom right to left moved a wild and gorgeous apparition of a woman.

She walked with measured steps, draped in striped and fringed cloths, treading the earth proudly, with a slight jingle and flash of barbarous ornaments. She carried her head high; her hair was done in the shape of a helmet; she had brass leggings to the knee, brass wire gauntlets to the elbow, a crimson spot on her tawny cheek, innumerable necklaces of glass beads on her neck; bizarre things, charms, gifts of witch-men, that hung about her, glittered and trembled at every step. She must have had the value of several elephant tusks upon her. She was savage and superb, wild-eyed and magnificent; there was something ominous and stately in her deliberate progress. And in the hush that had fallen suddenly upon the whole sorrowful land, the immense wilderness, the colossal body of fecund and mysterious life seemed to look at the image of its own tenebrous and passionate soul. (p. 99)

A cursory reading would probably suggest that this is a clear portrait of the woman. But the clarity of detail ('measured steps'; 'slight jingle'; 'crimson spot'; 'glass beads') is complicated by what seems to be a confusion of positives and negatives (or negative connotations): 'wild and gorgeous'; 'proudly'; 'barbarous'; 'She carried her head high; her hair was done in the shape of a helmet'; 'savage and superb'; 'wild-eyed and magnificent'; 'ominous and stately'. There is a sense that Marlow does not know what to make of this self-assured and regal woman. He was (and seems to still be) clearly fascinated by her (why else would he focus on her, and describe her, with such detail?) and his description, with its long, sibilant, sensuous sentences, hints at sexual desire. There presumably was not an actual 'hush'; Marlow's astonishment has made him block out all sounds that are not connected with her. The negative terms, however, could suggest that he is uneasy about both her and his response, not necessarily because she is African, but perhaps so.

The portrait of the African woman is often compared and contrasted by critics with the portrait of the Intended, perhaps reinforcing (whether intentionally or not) Chinua Achebe's assertion that 'she fulfils a structural requirement of the story: a savage counterpart to the refined, European woman who will step forth at the end of the story' (p. 6). It is, of course, necessary to consider Marlow's presentation of the two women, but it is also fruitful to compare his response to the African woman with his response to another 'apparition', the accountant at the Company's station:

> I met a white man, in such an unexpected elegance of get-up that in the first moment I took him for some sort of vision. I saw a high starched collar, white cuffs, a light alpaca jacket, snowy trousers, a clear silk necktie, and varnished boots. No

hat. Hair parted, brushed, oiled, under a green-lined parasol held in a big white hand. He was amazing, and had a pen-holder behind his ear.

[. . .] I respected the fellow. (p. 36)

There is the same attention to detail here as there is in the description of the African woman and Marlow is clearly also surprised by meeting this 'sort of vision', but there is nothing to suggest that he is troubled by it, presumably because the accountant is white, which he stresses: 'a white man'; 'a big white hand'. He also feels comfortable enough to express his feelings about the man – 'He was amazing'; 'I respected the fellow' – because they are asexual, which is reflected in the dry, at times stilted, prose.

The confusion of positive and negative terms regarding the African woman suggests a confused response, the negative terms suggesting unease, but it is noticeable that Marlow does not stress her blackness. But for the 'tawny cheek', she could be a white woman (we make her 'black'); and 'tawny' is in such stark contrast to his lazy use of monotypic 'black' in the descriptions of the men he has met on his journey to the Inner Station that there is something rather tender about it. Perhaps, then, Marlow's complicated response is not because she is African but because she has power: commanding status, commanding sexuality.

In her excellent feminist reading of the novel, '"Too Beautiful Altogether": Patriarchal Ideology in *Heart of Darkness*', Johanna M. Smith close-reads Marlow's description and, regarding its ending, notes:

The distancing language of [the final sentence] shows Marlow separating the woman herself from the material reality she represents for him: the 'body' of the jungle, outside her, looks not at her body or at its own 'soul' but at the '*image*' of its soul in her. Here Marlow symbolizes the woman and personifies the jungle, thereby confounding them and containing them both. (p. 184)

It might be argued, then, that Marlow, on the *Nellie* and perhaps at the time, (re)asserts his authority and displaces his unease by relating the woman to the jungle, transferring her from self to symbol, wood to woman.

It is possible, however, that 'the immense wilderness, the colossal body of fecund and mysterious life seemed to look at the image of its own tenebrous and passionate soul' emphasizes still further the woman's power and, in the light of Marlow's previous descriptions of the forest as a 'force' beyond his control (see, for example, pp. 59–60), exalts her and reaffirms his sense of inferiority. It is also possible that the supposedly negative terms – 'wild', 'barbarous', 'savage', 'wild-eyed', 'ominous' – are not negative. We might assume that they are; and that probably says something about us as readers: an African woman is negatively 'wild', 'barbarous', 'savage', 'wild-eyed' and 'ominous'. But there is no indication that 'wild', for example, is a denigrating judgement, especially when it is coupled with 'gorgeous' (a good dictionary, such as the *Oxford English Dictionary*, should always be used for words that might have more than one meaning). 'Ominous' is, in the context of the passage, negative, but it could say more about Marlow's sense of inferiority in the presence of the woman than it does about her.

It is perhaps also productive to think again about Conrad's use of the juxtaposition of scenes (see Chapter 3, on the 'grove of death' and the accountant). Marlow's journey to Kurtz has finally ended. Expectation has built. We are finally going to meet the great man himself, finally hear him talk. Kurtz appears, carried on a stretcher: 'He looked at least seven feet long. His covering had fallen off, and his body emerged from it pitiful and appalling as from a winding-sheet. I could see the cage of his ribs all astir, the bones of his arm waving' (p. 97). We eventually hear him say, 'I am glad', and are then probably baffled by Marlow's response: 'A voice! a voice! It was grave, profound, vibrating, while the man did not seem capable of a whisper' (p. 98). Kurtz is, for the reader, an anti-climax: all that way for a gangly, skinny man with nothing interesting to say. But we do get a climax: the African woman, on whom 'Conrad lavishes a whole page quite unexpectedly' (Achebe, p. 5). In contrast to Kurtz, she is vital, empowered, and stunning. She fulfils readerly expectations of significance at the end of the journey.

KURTZ'S WOMEN?

Achebe has a problem with her not speaking – 'It is clearly not part of Conrad's purpose to confer language on the "rudimentary souls" of Africa' (p. 6) – and it is possible to see this as a wilful act of dehumanization regarding some of the African characters (and some of the European). But with regard to the African woman, the silence Conrad gives her *here* is more thoughtful and meaningful than any words she could have spoken:

> She looked at us all as if her life had depended upon the unswerving steadiness of her glance. Suddenly she opened her bared arms and threw them up rigid above her head, as though in an uncontrollable desire to touch the sky, and at the same time the swift shadows darted out on the earth, swept along the river, gathering the steamer in shadowy embrace. A formidable silence hung over the scene. (pp. 99–100)

Her gesture is as haunting and as enigmatic as 'The horror! The horror!' (p. 112). And in its futility – she knows Kurtz is going to be taken from her – it is perhaps more upsetting. Kurtz knows he is about to die, so can escape the burden of knowledge; the woman does not have that blessing.

As the steamer leaves, taking Kurtz away from the Inner Station, there is on the slope leading down to the river:

> an eddy in the mass of human bodies, and the woman with helmeted head and tawny cheeks rushed out to the very brink of the stream. She put out her hands, shouted something, and all that wild mob took up the shout in a roaring chorus of articulated, rapid, breathless utterance. LANGUAGE
> 'Do you understand this?' I asked [Kurtz].
> He kept on looking past me with fiery, longing eyes, with a mingled expression of wistfulness and hate. He made no answer, but I saw a smile, a smile of indefinable meaning, appear on his colourless lips that a moment after twitched convulsively. 'Do I not?' (pp. 108–9)

What she says and what the others then chant is as 'indefinable' as Kurtz's smile, but whatever it was endows her with empathy –

western
science

it is presumably something she thinks Kurtz will want to hear –
and authority,[1] two things that the Intended seems to lack.

THE INTENDED

Back in Brussels, ill – feverish, delirious, on the verge of a mental
breakdown (p. 114) – and being looked after by his aunt, Marlow
contemplates 'the girl's portrait' that is in his possession, along
with 'a slim packet of letters':

> She struck me as beautiful – I mean she had a beautiful expres-
> sion. I know that the sunlight can be made to lie too, yet one felt
> that no manipulation of light and pose could have conveyed the
> delicate shade of truthfulness upon those features. She seemed
> ready to listen without mental reservation, without suspicion,
> without a thought for herself. I concluded I would go and give
> her back her portrait and those letters myself. Curiosity? Yes;
> and also some other feeling perhaps. (pp. 116–17)

This is a curious passage that raises doubts about Marlow and
his expectations. His distinction between 'beautiful' and 'beautiful expression' is unclear, and 'some other feeling perhaps' invites
speculation that he finds her sexually attractive.[2] Why he is not
more clear for the men on the *Nellie* might be that he is embar-
rassed to discuss such matters, or that he really did not know
what he felt. It is unlikely that the men would have been thinking
about how 'sunlight can be made to lie'. In saying so, even with
the following qualification, Marlow sows the possibility that the
portrait is untruthful. Furthermore, the uncertainty – 'I mean',
'one felt' (not 'one knew'), 'seemed', 'perhaps' – and the repetition – 'beautiful', 'light', 'without' – suggest that Marlow, in his
fragile, rather misanthropic, state was trying to convince himself
of her, pinning hope on her: turning her into a rivet to stop
himself descending further into Kurtzean nihilism.

He goes on to say:

> All that had been Kurtz's had passed out of my hands: his
> soul, his body, his station, his plans, his ivory, his career. There

remained only his memory and his Intended – and I wanted to give that up too to the past, in a way, – to surrender personally all that remained of him with me to that oblivion which is the last word of our common fate. I don't defend myself. I had no clear perception of what it was I really wanted. Perhaps it was an impulse of unconscious loyalty, or the fulfilment of one of those ironic necessities that lurk in the facts of human existence. I don't know. I can't tell. But I went. (p. 117)

Marlow wants to erase Kurtz and to do so requires him using the Intended.[3] But he is still, on the *Nellie*, confused and confusing. If his story is, as Robert Hampson suggests, 'a heuristic narration, driven by Marlow's desire to understand his own experience' (1992, p. 108), then his failure here and elsewhere to understand suggests that he is going to have to tell his story again, and again, and again, until 'the last word' – death.

When Marlow meets the Intended, she is unlike the woman in the portrait:

She came forward, all in black, with a pale head, floating towards me in the dusk. She was in mourning. It was more than a year since his death, more than a year since the news came; she seemed as though she would remember and mourn for ever. She took both my hands in hers and murmured, 'I had heard you were coming.' I noticed she was not very young – I mean not girlish. She had a mature capacity for fidelity, for belief, for suffering. [. . .] She carried her sorrowful head as though she were proud of that sorrow, as though she would say, I – I alone know how to mourn for him as he deserves. But while we were still shaking hands, such a look of awful desolation came over her face that I perceived she was one of those creatures that are not the playthings of Time. For her he had died yesterday. (pp. 118–19)[4]

When this passage is read out in class, there are always conflicting responses. Laughter is occasionally prompted by, 'with a pale head', which is certainly a rather strange expression ('face' would be expected), and a lad, remembering 'Curiosity? Yes; and also some other feeling perhaps', has been known to guffaw at, 'I had heard you were coming'. Significantly, though, students divide into those who feel sympathy for the Intended and those who do not. Those who do cite the length of her mourning ('more than a year since his death' is tragic) and the profundity of: 'she seemed as though she would remember and mourn for ever' and, 'For her he had died yesterday'. They also note that her grief has reduced her to a ghost, surrounded by 'dusk' rather than the sunshine of the portrait. They tend to agree that Marlow should comfort her. Those who do not sympathize with her cite the length of her mourning ('more than a year since his death' is ridiculous) and the absurdity of: 'she seemed as though she would remember and mourn for ever' and, 'For her he had died yesterday'. They also note that her grief has reduced her to a ghost, surrounded by 'dusk' rather than the sunshine of the portrait. They tend to agree that Marlow should tell her to pull herself together.

I usually find myself siding with the least sympathetic students, partly because the text prompts me to wonder how deep her mourning is: there is possibly an element of theatricality of wearing black for over a year, and of taking 'both hands in hers' and murmuring. This makes Marlow's 'seemed' – 'seemed as though she would remember and mourn for ever' – suggest 'seeming': an outward appearance that is deceptive.[5] My response is also partly influenced by Olivia in Shakespeare's *Twelfth Night*, who has decided to mourn the death of her brother for 'seven years' (1.1.25) but gets sidetracked by the witty and beautiful Cesario, and by my reading of the Polish and Czech poetry that emerged from the Holocaust, which, given the horror, is highly un-self-pitying (see Zbigniew Herbert, Miroslav Holub and Wisława Szymborska in Weissbort). It is valuable to stop and consider the extent to which our responses and interpretations are being influenced by past reading and, to put it simply, who we are. As discussed at the end of Chapter 3, New Historicism and cultural materialism remind us that the act of interpreting the past is never impersonal, objective or ahistorical, and that it is constructive to be aware of the place from which we read.

Nina Pelikan Straus, in her vigorously feminist essay 'The Exclusion of the Intended from Secret Sharing in Conrad's "Heart of Darkness"', discusses the 'autobiographical resonances' that are 'hidden within supposedly objective commentary' by 'mainstream [male] critics' (p. 124) and the differences between men's and women's responses to a novel whose 'artistic conventions [. . .] are brutally sexist' (p. 125).[6] Straus is no doubt correct to assert that women experience the novel differently from men, but then each man experiences the novel differently: Chinua Achebe's response to it, for example, is different from Cedric Watts's. Furthermore, there is not a neat gender split between the critics. Susan Jones states:

> Nina Pelikan Straus offers a useful reading of *Heart of Darkness*. She expresses the difficulties encountered by the woman reader of this novella, rightly observing that 'although [Marlow] speaks *about* women, there is no indication that women might be included among his hearers' [p. 124]. However, far from vindicating the exclusion of women from the text, I believe that Conrad's presentation of the Intended offers a critique of patriarchal structures that marginalise the European women of the novel. (p. 171)

Jones acknowledges that 'Straus, like Chinua Achebe on the issue of Conrad's representation of the Africans, raises an important question about reader-response',[7] but argues (very briefly): 'By having Marlow protect [the Intended] from the truth, Conrad exposes the patriarchal strategy that has traditionally excluded women from knowledge of men's affairs' (p. 172). Jones is, of course, referring to Marlow's lie:

> 'His last word – to live with,' she murmured. 'Don't you understand I loved him – I loved him – I loved him!'
> I pulled myself together and spoke slowly.
> 'The last word he pronounced was – your name.'
> I heard a light sigh, and then my heart stood still, stopped dead short by an exulting and terrible cry, by the cry of inconceivable triumph and of unspeakable pain. 'I knew it – I

was sure!' . . . She knew. She was sure. [. . .] I could not tell her.
It would have been too dark – too dark altogether. . . . (p. 123)

In support of Jones, one can refer back to Marlow's comment to
the men on the *Nellie* that the Intended was 'out of it – completely. They – the women I mean – are out of it – should be out
of it. We must help them stay in that beautiful world of their own,
lest ours gets worse' (p. 80), and even further back to: 'It's queer
how out of touch with truth women are' (p. 28). If Jones is
correct, Conrad is exposing Marlow (and patriarchy) as ignorant
and self-serving, necessarily perpetrating the hierarchical
dichotomy Man/Woman. (Marlow certainly feels free, as Jones
says, to tell the men on the *Nellie* the truth.) Elaine Showalter
supports this, stating, 'In keeping the truth about Kurtz from the
Intended, Marlow ensures the continuation of the double worlds
of men and women' (p. 98), but she does not suggest that Conrad
was being satirical.

'She knew. She was sure.' The Intended thinks she knows the
truth, but she does not. This invites the reader to wonder, especially in the light of the novel's presentation of epistemological
uncertainty: What if Marlow thinks he knows the truth, but he
does not? Perhaps he has a 'rotten apple' on his hands;[8] his certainty that he 'could not tell her' because it 'would have been too
dark' might be based on a falsehood: that women are weaker
than men, that they cannot handle the 'goodly apple' being
revealed as rotten. But perhaps not all women. A comparison
between the Intended and the African woman at the Inner
Station is prompted by Marlow: 'She put out her arms as if after
a retreating figure [. . .], resembling in this gesture another
["Shade"], tragic also, and bedecked with powerless charms,
stretching bare brown arms over the glitter of the infernal
stream, the stream of darkness' (p. 122). After the African's shout
and Kurtz's smile, 'the barbarous and superb woman did not so
much as flinch [at the steamer's whistle], and stretched tragically
her bare arms after us over the sombre and glittering river' (p.
109). Why 'tragically'? There is nothing to suggest that the
African woman's gesture is tragic; Marlow interprets it thus,
perhaps because he assumes that this is how a woman would act,

an assumption based on European patriarchal perceptions of (constructed) femininity. He seems to have forgotten (or is displacing) the image of self-assurance and power the African woman presented to him earlier.

Ruth Nadelhaft, in another feminist reading of the novel, suggests that by linking the African woman with the Intended, Marlow is 'fusing [. . .] two images into one yearning Woman' (p. 49). This would deny the Intended autonomy or power, yet the conversation between them can be read as her controlling Marlow: she certainly makes him (manoeuvres him?) into blurting: 'I heard his very last words. . . .' (p. 123).[9] It is easy to assume that 'the Intended' lacks any autonomy or power because of her 'name': 'it is difficult to refer to the woman whom Marlow meets at the end of the story other than by this term, which involves the critic in replicating her objectification and the subordination of her subjectivity to Kurtz's will' (Roberts 2000, p. 127).

When Marlow 'repeats' Kurtz's last words, it is interesting to note that the Intended gives a 'cry of inconceivable triumph' (p. 123). Marlow does not understand why she (assuming he is interpreting correctly) would give a 'cry of [. . .] triumph'. It is possible, as Thomas Dilworth argues, that 'In her cry she exults in the assurance that she possessed Kurtz to the very end' (p. 519). The extent and form of that possession is unclear, but if she believes that she possessed him, had some kind of power over him, then from her point of view she did. She might be his Intended, but he is her Intended.

Should Marlow have lied to her? Perhaps. Perhaps not.[10] Right/Wrong. Ignorance/Knowledge. *Heart of Darkness* has shown us that things are rarely black and white.

CONCLUSION: THROUGH THE CHARACTERS TO THE KEY THEMES AND ISSUES

It is easy to reject works of literature that are 'difficult', to feel that you cannot face putting in the time to get to grips with them. But imagine if all the texts you had to study were uncomplicated, if they were like the 'yarns of seamen', which 'have a direct simplicity, the whole meaning of which lies within the shell of a cracked nut' (p. 18). Being an intelligent individual, you would very soon get painfully bored. Furthermore, your essays would be boring to write and would not reflect your individual intelligence: 'The novel is about good and evil. There are good characters and there are evil characters. "Don't be evil" is its moral.' It is surely better to have texts that demand a bit more of us.

If a novel, play or poem confuses you, great. If it frustrates you, fantastic. Think about why it confuses you, why it frustrates you. You will then begin to work out how the text works. You will no doubt find that not everything can be pinned down, but that does not matter. If, for example, there is a word or a sentence or a scene that can be read in a variety of ways, all you need to do is show your awareness that the word, sentence or scene is open to different interpretations. Embrace the openness of the text rather than attempt to close it off.

This study of *Heart of Darkness* has hopefully illuminated aspects of what is undoubtedly a complex novel, but also sown the seeds for you to become an even more sophisticated interpreter of literary works. By engaging with the characters, from those on the Thames and in Brussels to those in Africa, the novel's key themes and issues have been discussed, but so too have various issues concerning how we interpret texts.

An engagement with the primary narrator, Marlow as a story-teller and the other men on the *Nellie*, for example, led to dis-cussions of reliability, trust, lying, interpretation, meaning, intentionality, uncertainty, indeterminacy, language, influence, imperialism, colonialism, ignorance, characterization, self-presentation, manipulation, the instability of truth, Conrad's readership, politics, polemic, 'active listeners', morality, and nineteenth-century doubt – issues that inform an understanding of the rest of the novel. It would have been far easier to just mention the *Nellie* and the frame narrative, then get on with the journey to Kurtz, but elaboration is more productive.

This study has hopefully also shown that it is productive to think about the minor characters and the function they serve in the text. Chapter 2 discusses how Conrad uses several characters in Brussels to foreground certain issues and to instil in the reader a sense of foreboding: see the doctor and the Company's chief. The main function of Marlow's aunt might be seen as her getting Marlow a job, but through her 'the idea of colonisation as a civilising mission' is foregrounded (Hampson 1992, p. 108). She also functions to introduce the theme of women and ignorance. The foregrounding of colonialism is reinforced by Marlow's anecdote about Freslevel, another character who is easy to ignore, and who also serves to introduce the themes of insanity and absurdity.

Whilst analysing the characters and thinking about what issues they raise and the themes they are connected with, I have used numerous secondary sources: books, essays and journal articles. (Given the wealth of printed material on the novel, it was unnecessary to use the internet, which meant I did not have to spend hours trying to find a few grains of wheat in a pile of chaff.) It is clear throughout this study that there are critics I agree with and critics I do not. They are equal, though, in my use of them: they are used to strengthen my critical position. You are taught by your tutors to think critically about primary texts (novels, poems and plays); you should also think critically about secondary texts (including this one) and feel free to disagree with the arguments they offer, but your disagreement must be supported by your detailed reading of the primary text. I challenge what Chinua Achebe says about Conrad, for example, because I think his interpretation of the novel is incorrect, and I use the novel to reveal why. Elaboration is, again, the key.

When dealing with literary characters it is inevitable that we respond to them as we do human beings. But we need to be careful, or we can find that we avoid engaging with possible interpretations. The Intended, for example, is a character who, perhaps more than any other in the novel, provokes a personal reaction that can close down the text. By thinking about why we are reacting to her as we do, we can start to be slightly more objective and thus re-open the text. New Historicism and cultural materialism remind us that complete objectivity is not possible, but it is better to aim at it than merely assert personal opinion. Having re-read and re-re-read the text, and taken into account what critics have said, you might then decide that your first response to a character matches your informed critical opinion of him or her.

This study mentions New Historicism and cultural materialism; it also draws on the writing of various feminist and postcolonial critics to show how the novel can be read in different ways. Engaging with different critical and theoretical positions helps to illuminate the text, but also prompts us to consider the validity of our own interpretations. They force us back to the novel to see if we have been misreading it, or at least overlooking possible meanings.

Ultimately, what I hope this study has done is show you the fruitfulness of engaging with the function and the complexity of the novel's characters, and the necessity of relating the characters to the themes and issues. I hope I have also shown that it is vital to undertake detailed close reading – to analyse and analyse. Your analysis may result in the conclusion that conclusions are impossible, that it is not possible to say for sure whether or not, for example, Marlow has a problem with women, but so be it. You do not have to discover a kernel – but you do need to show you looked for one.

NOTES

NOTES TO INTRODUCTION: AN OVERVIEW OF *HEART OF DARKNESS*

1 *Blackwood's Edinburgh Magazine* as a title was 'simplified in 1905 to *Blackwood's Magazine* after years of it being referred to as such' (Finkelstein, p. 3); you will find that most secondary sources use the popular title. In his letters, Conrad tends to refer to it as 'Maga'.
2 For a discussion of the textual history of the novel, see Michael and Berry (1980).
3 As someone dependent on publication for his income, the letters do offer an insight into Conrad's concern with 'shekels' (18 Dec. 1898; Conrad 1986, p. 132). On Conrad not being able to 'afford to be disdainful of popular taste', see Mulhern, p. 63.
4 For more on Barthes and the influence of his essay, 'The Death of the Author', on literary studies, see Jefferson and Robey (1991); Selden and Widdowson (1993).
5 For more on the limits that texts impose, see Iser (2000).
6 See Watts (1993), pp. 82–5, on the sun being finite and end-of-the-century nihilism.

NOTES TO CHAPTER 1: ON THE *NELLIE*

1 For astute discussions of a range of novel openings, from Daniel Defoe's *Robinson Crusoe* (1719) to Hanif Kureishi's *The Buddha of Suburbia* (1990), that illustrate why time should be spent analysing in detail the first few pages (and then subsequent pages) of a text, see Peter Childs, *Reading Fiction: Opening the Text* (2001).
2 The unnamed narrator in the opening of *Youth* states: 'There was a director of companies, an accountant, a lawyer, Marlow and myself. The director had been a *Conway* boy, the accountant had served four

years at sea, the lawyer – a fine crusted Tory, High Churchman, the best of old fellows, the soul of honour – had been chief officer in the P. & O. service in the good old days [. . .]. Marlow (at least I think that is how he spelt his name) told the story, or rather the chronicle, of a voyage' (Conrad 1995, p. 9).

3 The novel was, as discussed in the introduction, first published in three parts in *Blackwood's Magazine*, but for publication in *Youth: A Narrative; and Two Other Stories* (1902) Conrad could have dispensed with the tripartite structure; why he did not do so is unknown. In 'The Waltons: *Frankenstein's* Literary Family', I suggest that Walton is an aspiring novelist who turns Frankenstein's spoken narrative into a novel (similar to *Heart of Darkness*, the spoken stories, by Frankenstein and the Creature, are split into novelistic chapters for no obvious reason). It is possible that Conrad was influenced by Shelley's novel; perhaps the unnamed narrator is a (possibly flawed) novelist: *Heart of Darkness* certainly engages with issues of writing, narrating, and fiction and artifice, as discussed later in this chapter. Cedric Watts has argued that: 'we are dealing with a tale which is largely *about* the telling of a tale: about the responsibilities and difficulties of seeing truly, judging fairly and expressing adequately' (1977, p. 124).

4 'During the summer of 1891 Conrad visited his friend G. F. W. Hope in Stanford, Essex, and made two trips in Hope's yawl, the *Nellie*, along the Thames estuary' (Conrad 2000, p. 126, n. 1). We need to be careful with biographical information as it can reduce texts' polysemous nature; it is better to tease out texts' many meanings rather than reduce their content (and our discussions) to the life of their authors. Even if Conrad had in mind Stanford and his two trips when writing the opening, he leaves it uncertain where the fictional *Nellie* is, and that uncertainty is what should be pondered.

5 It is possible that Conrad was influenced by the opening of Charles Dickens's *Bleak House* (1853), about which Nicola Bradbury has written: 'The view of "London" closes in to the dark confines of Lincoln's Inn Hall, but then winds through the streets to a longer perspective over the Thames and out towards the coast of England, until both land and sky are unanchored and the text and its readers cast adrift, floating in surreal defiance of gravity like passengers in a gas-filled balloon stranded in "a nether sky of fog"' (Bradbury, p. xi). Hawthorn (1992) states: 'I suspect that Conrad's debt to [Dickens] is too extensive and too profound ever to be more than inadequately charted. [. . .] Conrad's fiction is packed with possible echoes from *Bleak House*' (p. 136).

6 Ford's *Joseph Conrad: A Personal Remembrance* (1924) is worth reading, especially part 3, where Ford discusses his and Conrad's ideas about literary technique; extracts are reprinted in Conrad (2006) and Ford (1995a).

7 In 'A Few Don'ts By An Imagiste' (March 1913), Ezra Pound states: 'Use no superfluous word, no adjective, which does not reveal something. Don't use such an expression as "dim lands of *peace*." It dulls the image' (Jones 1972, p. 131).

8 It is not unknown for novels to be deliberately, constructively repetitious: in *Pride and Prejudice* (1813), for example, 'pride', 'proud', 'proudest', 'fine', 'handsome', 'agreeable', 'disagreeable', 'good humoured' and 'accomplished' are repeated to the point of comicality, not because the novel is stylistically flawed or that Jane Austen was engaging in some sort of 'trickery', but to expose the limited views, concerns and language of the characters.

9 For an interesting, if undeveloped and rather idiosyncratic, discussion of the 'Adjectival Style in the *Fin de Siècle*', see Paul Coates, *The Double and the Other: Identity as Ideology in Post-Romantic Fiction* (1988), pp. 70–2.

10 Mulhern also states: 'Conrad's primary narrators are ill-placed to arbitrate, because they know little or nothing of what they now report at one remove' (p. 76).

11 In *Thorns & Arabesques* (1980), William W. Bonney says of the novel's ending: 'The narrator's final remark is inconclusive. It could involve simply the transposition of the diction he has heard for hours from Marlow onto his relating of the fact that during Marlow's tale the sun has set and it has grown dark: "The offing was barred by a black bank of clouds, and the tranquil waterway . . . seemed to lead into the heart of an immense darkness" [pp. 123–4]. The remark does not necessarily betray a completed "moral progress," although it may' (p. 155); 'moral progress' is quoted from Seymour Gross (1957), 'A further note on the function of the frame in "Heart of Darkness"', 170.

12 Parry (1983) also notes of the primary narrator: 'his testimony on Marlow as a guru is unsupported by Marlow's insistence on his partial knowledge and imperfect understanding, his groping a way towards comprehending events into which he had been drawn' (p. 26). Jakob Lothe has argued that: 'the personal narrator's opening remarks indicate a more unproblematic, simplifying attitude to the text's main thematic concerns than that of Marlow, whose story he transmits' (Knowles and Moore, p. 125).

13 *Youth: A Narrative; and Two Other Stories* (1902) 'is a volume with unity and design of a kind – an account of the Ages of Man, Conrad here keeping company with Aristotle in dividing man's life into three ages – youth, maturity (*Heart of Darkness*) and old age (*The End of the Tether*). The volume has a further unity in the tone, sceptical and sardonic, in which this grand archaic scheme of man's life is treated – the endeavour of *Youth* is a failure; maturity in *Heart of Darkness* is marked, not by enlightenment but by its opposite; and folly rather

than wisdom leads the elderly Captain Whalley to the end of his tether' (Lyon, p. xii).

14 Walter Pater, 'whom Conrad admired' (Watts 1993, p. 81), in his famous 'Conclusion' (first published as part of his 1868 essay, 'Poems by William Morris') to *The Renaissance* (1873), meditates on meaning, understanding and the relationship between the internal and external: 'And if we continue to dwell in thought on this world, not of objects in the solidity with which language invests them, but of impressions unstable, flickering, inconsistent, which burn and are extinguished with our consciousness of them, it contracts still further; the whole scope of observation is dwarfed to the narrow chamber of the individual mind. Experience, already reduced to a swarm of impressions, is ringed round for each one of us by that thick wall of personality through which no real voice has ever pierced on its way to us, or from us to that which we can only conjecture to be without. Every one of those impressions is the impression of the individual in his isolation, each mind keeping as a solitary prisoner its own dream of a world' (p. 235); an extract is reprinted in Kolocotroni *et al.*; see Watt (1980) on how such 'epistemological solipsism became an important part of the cultural atmosphere of the nineties' (p. 172).

A sense of epistemological darkness and limited enlightenment pervades modernist writing; see, for example, Ford Madox Ford, *The Good Soldier*: 'I don't know. And there is nothing to guide us. And if everything is so nebulous about a matter so elementary as the morals of sex, what is there to guide us in the more subtle morality of all other personal contacts, associations, and activities? Or are we meant to act on impulse alone? It is all a darkness' (p. 15); and Virginia Woolf, 'Modern Fiction', in *Collected Essays*: 'Life is not a series of gig-lamps symmetrically arranged; life is a luminous halo, a semi-transparent envelope surrounding us from the beginning of consciousness to the end' (p. 106).

15 Hampson (1992) suggests that Marlow's narration is 'driven by [his] desire to understand his own experience' (p. 108); Brooks argues, to simplify his fascinating thesis, that Marlow needs to retell Kurtz's story because he 'mistold [it] the first time' (to the Intended) (p. 255). For more on Marlow's prologue, see Berthoud, pp. 43–4; Fothergill, pp. 18–23; Hampson (1992), pp. 106–8; Parry, pp. 27–8; Ravel, pp. 20–3.

16 Bonney, p. 155, and Watts (1993), p. 91, note a parallel between Marlow's psychological problems and objection to people after his voyage and Gulliver's madness and abhorrence of his family when he returns to England; see Swift, pp. 338–9.

17 For further details, see Dilworth, pp. 510–13.

18 For more on Marlow's audience, see Stape and Knowles (2006).

19 For a brief discussion of modernist authorial impersonality, see Whitworth, pp. 64–5; on Conrad's 'withdrawal from the surface of his story', see Docherty, pp. 63–4.

NOTES TO CHAPTER 2: BEFORE THE CONGO

1 *Heart of Darkness* owes a debt to such stories, especially H. Rider Haggard's *King Solomon's Mines* (1886); for more on the Victorian adventure story, Conrad and imperialism, see Brantlinger (1988), (2004).
2 The statements 'most blank, so to speak' and 'got filled since my boyhood with rivers and lakes and names' draw attention to the European imperialist point of view: the arrogantly reductive 'blank spaces' are thus for the European, not their indigenous populations.
3 Towards the end of the passage on wanting as a boy to go to one of the 'blank spaces', Marlow states: 'The North Pole was one of these places, I remember. Well, I haven't been there yet, and shall not try now. The glamour's off' (p. 22). This might be a historical allusion, perhaps to the unsuccessful Polaris expedition (1871–72), or a literary allusion to Walton's expedition, which is highly unglamorous; much is still to be written about the influence of *Frankenstein* on *Heart of Darkness*.
4 See Brantlinger (1988) on 'New Imperialism', which began in the 1880s.
5 This foregrounds Kurtz as an idol and the 'unspeakable rites' (p. 83).
6 'Is it violence to impose our beliefs on children, who do not have the mental powers to resist? When we initiate children into our culture, we indoctrinate them; that is unavoidable. Should we say, then, that indoctrination can take two forms, good and bad, and that only the second of these should be described as violence? But if we distinguish between good and bad indoctrination on the basis of what we consider to be the right beliefs, principles and norms, then our definition of violence will be based on our own view of the world; and that surely will not do' (Kołakowski, pp. 81–2).
7 In his 'Preface to *The Nigger of the "Narcissus"*' (1897), Conrad states: 'My task which I am trying to achieve is, by the power of the written word, to make you hear, to make you feel – it is, before all, to make you *see*! That – and no more: and it is everything! If I succeed, you shall find there according to your desserts: encouragement, consolation, fear, charm – all you demand; and, perhaps, also that glimpse of truth for which you have forgotten to ask' (Conrad 1979, p. 147). In 'Conrad's Preface to *The Nigger of the "Narcissus"*', Ian Watt (1974) asserts that 'since [. . .] Conrad wrote no other equally inward account of his creative aspiration, the

Preface [. . .] remains by default the most reliable, and the most voluntary, single statement of Conrad's general approach to writing' (p. 153).

8 For an interesting discussion of humour and 'moral ambiguity' (p. 32) in the European novel, see Kundera, pp. 3–33; on Marlow's sense of humour allowing him to cope with the horror he witnesses, see William A. Corvino, 'Lugubrious Drollery: Humor and Horror in Conrad's Fiction', in Carabine, vol. 4.

9 For a detailed discussion of sticks, spears (Freleven is killed with a spear), point of view and 'delayed decoding', see Chapter 3.

10 Feder's interpretation of the women is part of her thesis that, throughout the novel, Conrad 'employs the imagery and symbolism of the traditional voyage into Hades. By associating Marlow's journey with the descent into hell [especially as described in Virgil's *Aeneid*], Conrad concretizes the hidden world of the inner self. Through image and symbol, he evokes the well-known voyage of the hero who, in ancient epic, explores the lower world and, in doing so, probes the depths of his own and his nation's conscience' (p. 280). Feder's overall thesis is rather too neat for such an untidy (complicated and often contradictory) novel, but she does raise many interesting points, especially about Kurtz and the Intended, that can be used without their links to past literature.

11 There is not space in this study to engage with all that Watt says about Conrad, the novel and symbolism; spending time reading *Conrad in the Nineteenth Century* will be time well spent.

12 Marlow's meeting with the head of the Company does not instil confidence in the organization or optimism in Marlow's future: 'From behind that structure came out an impression of pale plumpness in a frock-coat. The great man himself. He was five feet six, I should judge, and had his grip on the handle-end of ever so many millions. He shook hands, I fancy, murmured vaguely, was satisfied with my French. *Bon voyage*' (p. 25).

13 See Conrad (2002), pp. 205–6, n. 112; Greenslade, p. 113; Griffith, p. 160; Watts (1993), pp. 92–3.

14 See Griffith, pp. 161–3; Watts (1993), p. 92.

15 See 'Degeneration and Crime', in Stevenson (2000); 'Degeneration', in Stoker.

NOTES TO CHAPTER 3: ON THE CONGO

1 See Conrad (2002), p. 206, n. 113. For more on Stanley and King Leopold II of Belgium, who rather underhandedly used Stanley to ensure that the Congo basin became a Belgian colony, see Baines, pp. 106–7; Hampson (2000), pp. xvi–xxii.

2 Hampson (1992) states: 'Civilising the Africans means making them

slaves and working them till they die, and the soldiers and agents who supervise this "heavenly mission" are as exploited as the Africans' (p. 108); 'as exploited' is presumably an exaggeration, given what we soon witness of the treatment of the black slaves.

3 The terms 'signifier' and 'signified' are Ferdinand de Saussure's, the Swiss philologist and professor of linguistics whose *Cours de Linguistique Générale* was published posthumously in 1915. Saussure suggested that language is a system of signs, and that a sign is 'the union of two elements, a sound-image (or its written substitute) and a concept; for the first the term *signifier* is used, for the second *signified* (*signifiant* or *signifié*). For instance, the sound "tree" that I hear is the signifier, to which there corresponds a signified *tree* in the sense of the concept that the sound evokes in my mind' (Jefferson and Robey, p. 47).

4 See also the 'objectless blasting' of a cliff that 'was not in the way or anything' (pp. 32–3); 'Some editors emend this to "in the way of anything", the manuscript reading' (Conrad 1995, p. 307, n. 28). Also the 'vast artificial hole somebody had been digging on the slope, the purpose of which I found impossible to divine' (p. 34) and the bucket with 'a hole in the bottom' (p. 44).

5 For more on the 'linguistic theme' of Marlow's narrative, see Watts (1993), p. 129. Euphemism is discussed later in this chapter.

6 Chinua Achebe quotes a section of this passage and dismisses Marlow's 'bleeding-heart sentiments' and 'liberalism' (p. 7), which suggests that Achebe did not spend much time analysing it. For more on Achebe's response to the passage, see Watts (1983), pp. 201–2. Achebe is also discussed later in this chapter and in Chapter 5.

7 The term 'devil' recurs throughout the novel; see, for example, pp. 34, 40, 49, 51, 70, 79, 81. Contemporary with *Heart of Darkness* are Bram Stoker's *Dracula* (1897) and Henry James's *The Turn of the Screw* (1898), which similarly problematize the binary oppositions of 'innocent' and 'guilty', 'good' and 'evil', 'devil' and 'angel'.

8 Hampson (1992) writes of Marlow's 'ironic tone' (p. 109); Watt (1980) of Marlow reflecting 'half ironically' (p. 221).

9 Schwarz states: 'The more [Marlow] became disillusioned, the more Kurtz became the goal of his quest' (p. 66); Hawthorn (1992): 'Marlow wants to see whether Kurtz *can* unite idealism and successful trade – or imperialism' (p. 177).

10 For more on Marlow's suspicions about 'the real significance of that wreck', part of what Cedric Watts calls the novel's 'covert plot', see Watts (1984); Watts (1993), pp. 119-20. Hawthorn (1992), pp. 174–7, uses Watts to discuss this section of the novel, readerly uncertainty and Marlow's growing interest in Kurtz.

11 The phrase is Ford Madox Ford's; writing in *Mightier Than the Sword* (1938) about the collapse of certainty at the start of the

twentieth century, Ford states: 'it is characteristic of a confused world dominated by a hybrid social stratum that of necessity never had any use for the Big Words . . . that along with the disappearance of Continence, Probity, and the belief in revealed religion, Truth should have developed the bewildering faculty of the chameleon and have taken on like Janus, two faces. . . . There is no longer one Faith, no longer any one Cause, no longer any one anything for the reasoning man' (p. 235). In *Some Do Not* . . ., the main protagonist, Christopher Tietjens, says: 'Principles are like the skeleton map of a country – you know whether you're going east or north' (*Parade's End*, p. 144).

12 For more on this view, its historical context and Conrad's pessimism, see the introduction; Watt (1980); Watts (1993).

13 Shoshana Felman reinforces this view: 'the metaphysical logic of dichotomous oppositions which dominates philosophical thought (Presence/Absence, Being/Nothingness, Truth/Error, Same/Other, Identity/Difference, etc.) is, in fact, a subtle mechanism of hierarchisation which assures the unique valorisation of the "positive" pole (that is, of a *single* term) and, consequently, the repressive subordination of all "negativity", the mastery of difference as such' (p. 135). Thus, 'Presence', for example, or 'Masculine' are prioritized and given value above 'Absence' and 'Feminine'. The same could be said for 'White' and 'Black'.

14 Jacques Berthoud writes that the cannibals' restraint 'sets them above the very moralists who condemn them' (p. 48).

15 Allan H. Simmons argues that the 'passage is condescending, paternalistic, and resonates with ethnocentric clichés, yet it consistently upsets our expectations through qualifications and tonal shifts'; he also mentions 'Marlow's racist canine comparison' (p. 95).

16 For more information, see Hawkins (2006).

17 Brantlinger (1988), Sarvan (Conrad 1988), Singh (Conrad 1988) and Torgovnick (Conrad 2006) are examples of critics writing on *Heart of Darkness* in the light of Achebe. Recent guides to literary criticism and theory now contain discussions of postcolonialism; see, for example, Bennett and Royle, pp. 214–22, which also discusses *Heart of Darkness*. Suggested further reading includes Ashcroft *et al.* (1995), (2002); McLeod (2000).

18 For more on Marlow, work and seamanship, see Hampson (1992), pp. 112–14.

19 Regarding Marlow's assertion of kinship, William Greenslade writes: 'Rather than repress this affiliation in the interests of difference, power or fear, Conrad has Marlow offer atavism as a constituent part of a common heritage and a common experience. It is an insight which marks a decisive shift away from the hierarchical assumptions which late nineteenth-century positivism

underpinned and which issued in imperial conquest and suppression' (p. 65).

20 For more information, see Selden and Widdowson, pp. 161–9; McGann, pp. 111–32; Veeser (1989).

NOTES TO CHAPTER 4: AT THE INNER STATION

1 There are many instances of delayed decoding in Conrad's work, including: 'Wait!', which is taken to mean a command to halt but is then understood to be someone's name (p. 10), in *The Nigger of the 'Narcissus'* (1897); 'a queer sensation', which eventually becomes 'Coals, gas! – By Jove! we are being blown up', in *Youth* (1995, p. 26); and 'something round and enormous, resembling a sixteen-hundred-weight sugar-hogshead wrapped in striped flannelette', which turns out to be a man (p. 38), in *Lord Jim* (1899–1900). For other examples, see Watt (1980), pp. 175–6; Watts (1984), pp. 44–6.

2 There can be a significant delay in the decoding, for example the 'round carved balls' on posts (p. 86) are later understood to be 'heads' (p. 94). Cedric Watts (1984, p. 45) also cites the 'notes pencilled in the margin' of *An Inquiry into Some Points of Seamanship*, which Marlow sees as 'cipher' (code; pp. 65, 89) but later understands is Russian (p. 89). Watts extends 'delayed decoding' to apply to 'longer narrative sequences' (such as the 'covert murder plot' of the novel) and 'ultimately to the narrative strategies of whole works: as in *Heart of Darkness*, where we have to interpret Marlow's own reported attempt to decipher and comprehend the meaning of the journey into the Congo which he is recalling' (p. 45). Disrupting linear chronology can also be seen as a type of delayed decoding: the reader can witness an incident (an effect) but not know its cause; only from further reading, going back in narrative time, might a cause be given, allowing for decoding to take place. Conrad utilizes this to great effect in *Nostromo* (1904); for more information, see Guerard, p. 175.

3 Simplifying (greatly) Watt's brilliant discussion does not do it justice; you are encouraged to read 'Impressionism' (pp. 169–80) in his chapter on *Heart of Darkness*. Literary impressionism is a complex and rather contentious area in literary studies (J. A. Cuddon says that 'impressionist' and 'impressionism' 'are vague terms which we might well dispense with' (p. 446)), and it is unnecessary to go into detail in this study; to know more, begin with Knowles and Moore, pp. 188–90, then see Ford (1924), (1995b); Johnson (1985); Hay (1979); Matz (2001); Peters (2003). As well as Conrad, notable literary impressionists include Stephen Crane, Ford Madox Ford and Henry James.

4 See also the discussion in Chapter 1 on how each reader perceives and determines the 'haze' differently, and in Chapter 3 on Marlow slipping into a solipsistic, epistemologically uncertain world.

5 In *The Modes of Modern Writing*, David Lodge examines the main differences between modernist writing and realist writing; he notes that realist fiction by, for example, Jane Austen, Charles Dickens and George Eliot 'is based on the assumption that there is a common phenomenal world that may be reliably described' (p. 47). Compare the impressionistic view from the *Nellie* with the opening of Eliot's *The Mill on the Floss* (1860): 'A wide plain, where the broadening Floss hurried on between green banks to the sea, and the loving tide, rushing to meet it, checks its passage with an impetuous embrace', etc. (p. 53).

6 The phrase is Ford Madox Ford's, from *It Was the Nightingale* (1933): 'beneath Ordered Life itself was stretched, the merest film with, beneath it, the abysses of Chaos' (p. 49).

7 See Johnson, p. 53.

8 In 'On Impressionism', Ford states: 'any piece of Impressionism, whether it be prose, or verse, or painting, or sculpture, is the record of the impression of the moment; it is not a sort of rounded, annotated record of a set of circumstances' (1995b, p. 263).

9 It must be remembered that many of the negative statements about Kurtz are based on what Marlow hears and witnesses at the Inner Station. Marlow's story does not, therefore, follow exactly the chronology of his journey up the Congo; see n. 2, above. In *Joseph Conrad*, Ford discusses how he and Conrad agreed that: 'the general effect of a novel must be the general effect that life makes on mankind. A novel does not say to you: In 1914 my next door neighbour, Mr. Slack, erected a greenhouse and painted it with Cox's green aluminium paint. . . . If you think about the matter you will remember, in various unordered pictures [. . .]' (pp. 180–1).

10 For more on the painting, see Ravel, p. 29.

11 Lionel Trilling states correctly: 'It is scarcely possible to describe the character of Kurtz at once summarily and accurately' (p. 105). Trilling's chapter on Conrad in *Sincerity and Authenticity* contains several interesting, if contentious, ideas, and is worth reading; he views the novel as 'the paradigmatic literary expression of the modern concern with authenticity' (p. 106) and argues that Kurtz has 'the right to affirm the authenticity of life, which he did by articulating its horror' (p. 133). For more on Conrad and 'authenticity' (and Trilling), see Vidan (1992).

12 Similar to Kurtz, the Russian is, according to Marlow, 'an insoluble problem' (p. 90). For more on the Russian, see Hawthorn (1992), pp. 192–4; Hawthorn argues convincingly that 'the Russian's role in *Heart of Darkness* is to exemplify the fatal attraction that pure ideal-

ism can present to a particular kind of *man*; one naïve, disinterested and romantic' (p. 192).

13 This is a possible echo of a scene in H. Rider Haggard's *King Solomon's Mines* (1886), where, to astound (and overawe) a 'party of natives', in south-eastern Africa, Allan Quatermain shoots an antelope 'with a noise' (p. 105) – his rifle. In his report for the 'International Society for the Suppression of Savage Customs', Kurtz states, regarding 'whites' and the 'savages': 'we approach them with the might as of a deity' (p. 83).

14 Regarding the twentieth-century French theorist Michel Foucault, whose works include *Madness and Civilization* (1961), *The Birth of the Clinic* (1963) and *The Order of Things* (1966), Selden and Widdowson summarize that Foucault 'shows that social and political power works through discourse. For example, certain dichotomies are imposed as definitive of human existence and are operated in ways which have direct effects on society's organization. Discourses are produced in which concepts of madness, criminality, sexual abnormality, and so on are defined in relation to concepts of sanity, justice and sexual normality. Such discursive formations massively determine and constrain the forms of knowledge, the types of "normality" and the nature of "subjectivity" which prevail in particular periods' (p. 164). For more on Conrad's challenging of dichotomies in the novel, see Chapter 3.

15 I am drawing here on Stephen Dedalus in James Joyce's *A Portrait of the Artist as a Young Man* (1914): 'When the soul of man is born in this country [Ireland] there are nets flung at it to hold it back from flight. You talk to me of nationality, language, religion. I shall try to fly by those nets' (p. 171).

16 From 'Two Loves' (1896) by Lord Alfred Douglas, Oscar Wilde's lover.

17 For a discussion of narrative 'gaps' (and 'triggers'), see Wolfgang Iser, 'The Reading Process: A Phenomenological Response'. Iser argues that a text's 'gaps' (places of openness, uncertainty, ambiguity, where expectations are unfulfilled) give readers the opportunity to 'fill' them with their own interpretations, in a sense become a writer; 'each individual will fill in the gaps in his own way' (p. 193); 'The manner in which the reader experiences the text will reflect his own disposition, and in this respect the literary text acts as a kind of mirror' (p. 194).

18 In 'Conrad and the Psychology of Colonialism', Hunt Hawkins correctly points out that 'Kurtz's initial motive in going to the Congo seems to have been the desire to make money and rise in the European social scale' (p. 80) because of the Intended's family; Marlow learns from her that 'her engagement with Kurtz had been disapproved by her people. He wasn't rich enough or something.

And indeed I don't know whether he had not been a pauper all his life. He had given me some reason to infer that it was his impatience of comparative poverty that drove him out there' (p. 120).

19 I do not discuss the parallels between Marlow and Kurtz, or the possibility that Kurtz is Marlow's double; see Billy, pp. 69–77; Childs (2001), p. 81; Showalter, p. 96; Watts (1993), pp. 90–3.

20 Ted Billy argues that the 'The horror!' might not have been Kurtz's final words: 'Marlow was dining in the mess room at the time of [Kurtz's] death. It is possible that in his delirium Kurtz could have spoken anything without being overheard' (p. 73). This is unlikely, given the significance of Marlow's blowing out of the candle (p. 112). See also (among others) Berthoud, pp. 58–61; Brooks, pp. 238–63; Greaney, pp. 74–6; Hawthorn (1992), pp. 194–7; Ravel, pp. 34–6. For more on Kurtz further to these and the texts cited in this chapter, begin with: Adams, pp. 65–9; Brantlinger (1988), pp. 267–74; Greenslade, pp. 113–14; Griffith, pp. 161–5; Knowles (1994); Maier-Katkin and Maier–Katkin (2004); Parry, pp. 20–39; Watt (1980), pp. 161–8; Watts (1993), *passim*; Watts (2000), pp. 45–62. Peter Brooks mentions the nineteenth-century deathbed scene as representing 'the moment of summing-up of a life's meaning and a transmission of accumulated wisdom to succeeding generations' (p. 246) and discusses 'The horror! The horror!' as being 'as close as articulated speech can come to the primal cry' (p. 250): it 'stands on the verge of non-language, of non-sense' (p. 252). Brooks does not reference specific nineteenth-century deathbed scenes; in antithesis to Kurtz, see, for example, Prince Andrei in Leo Tolstoy's *War and Peace* (1865–69) – 'Sympathy, love of our brothers, for those who love us and for those who hate us, love of our enemies – yes, the love that God preached on earth, that Princess Maria tried to teach me and I did not understand – that is what made me sorry to part with life, that is what remained for me had I lived. But now it is too late. I know it!' (p. 968) – and Ralph Touchett in Henry James's *The Portrait of a Lady* (1880–81; 1908): 'Were we born to rot in our misery – were we born to be afraid? I never knew *you* afraid! If you'll only trust me, how little you will be disappointed! The world's all before us – and the world's very big. I know something about that' (p. 489). For further information, see Michael Wheeler, *Death and the Future Life in Victorian Literature and Theology*.

NOTES TO CHAPTER 5: KURTZ'S WOMEN?

1 Regarding the passage where the Russian describes the African woman talking 'like a fury to Kurtz' (p. 100), Thomas Dilworth (1987) notes that 'she is certainly used to influencing, maybe even dominating, Kurtz. [. . .] The Russian implies that usually when the

woman harangues Kurtz, Kurtz does as she says' (pp. 511, 512). I have in this study refrained from referring to the African woman as 'Kurtz's mistress': it is possible that they were in a sexual relationship, but it is equally possible that they were not; 'Kurtz's mistress' is also dismissive and undermines the status and autonomy she possesses; she seems to possess rather than be possessed. For more on the African woman, see Hawthorn (1992), pp. 183–92; Hyland, pp. 8–9; Nadelhaft, pp. 46–9; Smith, pp. 184–8.

2 This statement is glossed as: 'Conrad told [the literary adviser in Blackwood's London office] David Meldrum [in a letter of 2 January 1899] that *Heart of Darkness* offered "A mere shadow of love interest just in the last pages"' (p. 139, n. 115); 'love' could mean 'sexual'. In a letter (31 May 1902) to William Blackwood (editor of *Blackwood's Magazine*) Conrad wrote: 'I beg to instance [. . .] the last pages of Heart of Darkness where the interview of the man and the girl locks in – as it were – the whole 30000 words of narrative description into one suggestive view of a whole phase of life and makes of that story something quite on another plane than an anecdote of a man who went mad in the Centre of Africa' (Conrad 1986, p. 417). As with autobiographies and biographies, letters need to be treated with extreme caution, especially when they are from an author to a publisher, and especially when they concern matters of intention and/or interpretation. Just because Conrad thinks that the interview 'locks in' and 'makes of that story something quite on another plane' does not mean that it does.

3 For another reading of the passage, see Roberts (2000), pp. 129–30.

4 For an interesting discussion of the women in the novel being associated with drapery (and 'deception and covering'), see Childs (2001), p. 82.

5 Dilworth argues that the Intended 'may be a kind of lie' as she resembles 'a stock Romantic heroine, a product of conventional imagining and therefore an obvious fiction' (p. 518), but he sees the fiction as being created by Marlow in his recreation of the scene.

6 Straus's essay contains a useful overview of much significant (masculine) writing on the novel; see also Hyland (1988), who includes a discussion of Victorian patriarchal structure.

7 For introductions to reader-response theory, see Selden and Widdowson, pp. 46–69; Maclean (1991).

8 See the discussion in Chapter 4 on delayed decoding.

9 Mulhern offers another interpretation, which gives Marlow control: 'He conveys his truthful evaluation in words he knows she will translate into her illusion, which will thus persist as the authorized version. His tale, on this occasion, is a masterpiece of non-communication' (p. 80). Nadelhaft discusses 'Marlow's sardonic and manipulative

treatment of the woman from the first moments of their meeting' (p. 48).

10 For further discussions of the lie, see Berthoud, pp. 61–3; Hampson (1992), pp. 115–16; Hawthorn (1992), pp. 183–92; Hyland, pp. 3–11; Smith, pp. 190–5; Watt (1980), pp. 241–53.

GUIDE TO FURTHER READING

The annotated list that follows gives guidance on *some* of the texts you are likely to find useful when undertaking further research on *Heart of Darkness* and Conrad. It should be supplemented by the Bibliography.

PRIMARY TEXTS

Conrad, Joseph (1988), *Heart of Darkness* (3rd edn). Robert Kimbrough (ed.). New York and London: Norton.
Contains a wealth of material that illuminates the historical context and Conrad's life and opinions (including his essential statement on his writing, 'Preface to *The Nigger of the "Narcissus"*'), and an excellent selection of essays and extracts.
Conrad, Joseph (1989), *'Heart of Darkness': A Case Study in Contemporary Criticism*. Ross C. Murfin (ed.). New York: St Martin's Press.
The essays in Part 2 show how *Heart of Darkness* can be read in different ways; it covers topics such as psychoanalytic criticism, reader-response, feminism, deconstruction and New Historicism.
Conrad, Joseph (1995), *'Youth', 'Heart of Darkness', 'The End of the Tether'*. John Lyon (ed.). London: Penguin.
It is interesting to see how Conrad develops the function of the primary narrator between *Youth* and *Heart of Darkness* and to read the volume as 'an account of the Ages of Man' (Introduction, p. xii).

Conrad, Joseph (1996), *Heart of Darkness*. D. C. R. A. Goonetilleke (ed.). Ontario: Broadview.
Useful for its introduction and appendices: 'Comments by Conrad'; 'Contemporary Reviews'; 'Historical Documents'; 'Major Textual Changes'.
Conrad, Joseph (2002), *'Heart of Darkness' and Other Tales*. Cedric Watts (ed.). Oxford: Oxford University Press.
Contains 'An Outpost of Progress' (1897), which 'offers a ruthlessly ironic view of European colonialism and the pretensions of civilization' (Introduction, p. xi), and a useful introduction and bibliography.
Conrad, Joseph (2006), *Heart of Darkness* (4th edn). Paul B. Armstrong (ed.). New York and London: Norton.
A revised edition of Conrad (1988) and as invaluable for the Conrad scholar as the earlier edition.

SECONDARY TEXTS

Achebe, Chinua (1988), *Hopes and Impediments: Selected Essays 1965–1987*. Oxford: Heinemann.
Contains Achebe's controversial essay, 'An Image of Africa: Racism in Conrad's *Heart of Darkness*', which is best read alongside Brantlinger (1988), Greaney (2002), Hawthorn (1992), Watts (1983), and several essays in Conrad (1988) and Conrad (2006), both of which also contain Achebe.
Berthoud, Jacques (1978), *Joseph Conrad: The Major Phase*. Cambridge: Cambridge University Press.
Gives an illuminating and sensitive close reading of *Heart of Darkness*.
Brantlinger, Patrick (1988), *Rule of Darkness: British Literature and Imperialism, 1830–1914*. Ithaca and London: Cornell University Press.
Discussing race (and Achebe's essay; see above), imperialism and the novel's polysemy, Brantlinger offers a stimulating, if still provocative, reading of *Heart of Darkness*; extracts reprinted in Conrad (2006).
Brooks, Peter (1992), *Reading for the Plot: Design and Intention in Narrative*. Cambridge, MA: Harvard University Press.

Chapter 9, 'An Unreadable Report: Conrad's *Heart of Darkness*', is essential reading for anyone interested in the novel's structure, the primary narrator, Marlow and Kurtz; reprinted in Conrad (2006).

Dilworth, Thomas (1987), 'Listeners and Lies in *Heart of Darkness*'. *Review of English Studies* (new series), 38.152, 510–22.

Excellent on Marlow's lies, the Intended and the 'active influence of listeners on speakers' (p. 510).

Ford, Ford Madox (1924), *Joseph Conrad: A Personal Remembrance*. London: Duckworth.

Written by Conrad's friend and collaborator, Part 3 is of special interest: Ford discusses his and Conrad's ideas about literary technique; extracts reprinted in Conrad (2006) and Ford (1995a).

Greaney, Michael (2002), *Conrad, Language, and Narrative*. Cambridge: Cambridge University Press.

Excellent on Marlow; offers considered criticism of Achebe's essay (see above).

Hampson, Robert (1992), *Joseph Conrad: Betrayal and Identity*. Basingstoke: Macmillan; New York: St Martin's Press.

The section on *Heart of Darkness* illuminates many key passages in the novel and encourages detailed analysis of other passages.

Hawthorn, Jeremy (1992), *Joseph Conrad: Narrative Technique and Ideological Commitment*. London: Edward Arnold.

Two sections are particularly interesting: 'Seeing and Believing: Represented Speech and Thought in Conrad's Fiction' and '*Heart of Darkness*', which demonstrates perfectly how to combine detailed close reading of a text with an engagement with critics; extracts reprinted in Conrad (2006).

Knowles, Owen, and Gene M. Moore (2006), *Oxford Reader's Companion to Conrad*. Oxford: Oxford University Press.

An A–Z reference work containing informative entries on a wide range of subjects, including: 'Congo'; 'frame-narrative'; 'impressionism'; 'Kurtz'; 'Marlow'; and 'transtextual narratives'; short essays are supplied on the major fiction. A good starting point for further research and reflection.

Leavis, F. R. (1983), *The Great Tradition: George Eliot, Henry James, Joseph Conrad*. Harmondsworth: Penguin.
An influential book on Conrad studies, it contains Leavis's famous statement about Conrad's 'adjectival insistence' (p. 204).

Levenson, Michael H. (1992), *A Genealogy of Modernism: A Study of English Literary Doctrine 1908–1922*. Cambridge: Cambridge University Press.
Do not be intimidated by the title; this is one of the best discussions of early modernism. Conrad figures strongly in the first two chapters, 'Consciousness' and 'Authority'.

Lodge, David (1993), *The Modes of Modern Writing: Metaphor, Metonymy, and the Typology of Modern Literature*. London: Edward Arnold.
Another excellent book with a rather daunting title. Lodge discusses the differences between realist and modernist fiction; pp. 45–6 contain a useful summary of the key features of the latter.

Middleton, Tim (2006), *Joseph Conrad*. London: Routledge.
Discusses the evolution of critical responses to Conrad's fiction, from early reviews to the present day.

Moore, Gene M. (ed.) (2004), *Joseph Conrad's 'Heart of Darkness': A Casebook*. Oxford: Oxford University Press.
Contains a wide range of essays, notably Ian Watt's 'Conrad's Impressionism' and Nina Pelikan Straus's 'The Exclusion of the Intended from Secret Sharing in Conrad's *Heart of Darkness*' (see below).

Murfin, Ross C. (ed.) (1985), *Conrad Revisited: Essays for the Eighties*. Alabama: University of Alabama Press.
Contains J. Hillis Miller's '*Heart of Darkness* Revisted' (reprinted in Conrad (1989)) and Bruce Johnson's 'Conrad's Impressionism and Watt's "Delayed Decoding"' (reprinted in Conrad (1988)).

Nadelhaft, Ruth L. (1991), *Joseph Conrad*. Hemel Hempstead: Harvester Wheatsheaf.
Part of Harvester Wheatsheaf's 'Feminist Readings' series, its lucid discussions of Marlow and women offer a more considered approach than Straus (see below).

Parry, Benita (1983), *Conrad and Imperialism: Ideological Boundaries and Visionary Frontiers*. London: Macmillan.
Excellent on the primary narrator, Marlow and imperialism.
Roberts, Andrew Michael (2000), *Conrad and Masculinity*. Basingstoke: Macmillan; New York: St Martin's Press.
Chapter 5, 'Epistemology, Modernity and Masculinity: "Heart of Darkness"', elaborates a thesis on '(social) structures of male power and (psychic) structures of male desire' (p. 121). Roberts's suggestion that Kurtz's 'unspeakable rites' might have involved buggery is an interesting, if contentious, one (p. 133); extracts reprinted in Conrad (2006).
Schwarz, Daniel R. (1980), *Conrad: 'Almayer's Folly' to 'Under Western Eyes'*. Basingstoke: Macmillan.
Contains 'Marlow's Role in "Youth" and "Heart of Darkness"'.
Stape, J. H. (ed.) (2000), *The Cambridge Companion to Joseph Conrad*. Cambridge: Cambridge University Press.
Contains a range of essays, including: Owen Knowles, 'Conrad's Life'; Cedric Watts, '"Heart of Darkness"'; Jakob Lothe, 'Conradian Narrative'; Andrea White, 'Conrad and Imperialism'; Kenneth Graham, 'Conrad and Modernism'.
Straus, Nina Pelikan (1987), 'The Exclusion of the Intended from Secret Sharing in Conrad's *Heart of Darkness*'. *Novel: A Forum on Fiction*, 20.2, 123–37.
An essay born, in part, out of a concern with how 'the feminist reader has been traumatized by decades of nearly exclusive male commentary surrounding *Heart of Darkness*' (p. 198). Parts are unintentionally funny in their passionate hyperbole, but it is still a valuable and thought-provoking essay; reprinted in Moore (2004).
Watt, Ian (1980), *Conrad in the Nineteenth Century*. London: Chatto & Windus.
Still one of the best books on Conrad, this study illuminates Conrad's work and its historical context, and contains Watt's influential discussion of 'delayed decoding'; extracts reprinted in Conrad (1988) and Conrad (2006).
Watts, Cedric (1983), 'A Bloody Racist': About Achebe's View of Conrad'. *Yearbook of English Studies*, 13, 196–209.
One of the great Conrad scholars, Watts, responding to Achebe's

essay (see above), attempts 'to defend Conrad's tale from some of [Achebe's] strictures and discuss the criteria involved' (p. 196).

Watts, Cedric (1993), *A Preface to Conrad* (2nd edn). London: Longman; Harlow: Pearson Education.

The lack of detailed references for some of the quotations can be rather frustrating, but this is still one of the best introductions to Conrad's life, cultural background and art.

BIBLIOGRAPHY

PRIMARY TEXTS

Arnold, Matthew (1995), *The Works of Matthew Arnold*. Martin Corner (ed.). Ware: Wordsworth.

Austen, Jane (1998), *Pride and Prejudice*. James Kinsley (ed.). Oxford: Oxford University Press.

Beckett, Samuel (2000), *Waiting for Godot*. London: Faber and Faber.

Brontë, Charlotte (1985), *Jane Eyre*. Q. D. Leavis (ed.). Harmondsworth: Penguin.

Conrad, Joseph (1958), *Letters to William Blackwood and David S. Meldrum*. Durham, NC: Duke University Press.

Conrad, Joseph (1969), *Joseph Conrad's Letters to R. B. Cunninghame Graham*. C. T. Watts (ed.). Cambridge: Cambridge University Press.

Conrad, Joseph (1979), *The Nigger of the 'Narcissus'*. Robert Kimbrough (ed.). New York: Norton.

Conrad, Joseph (1983), *Lord Jim*. John Batchelor (ed.). Oxford: Oxford University Press.

Conrad, Joseph (1983), *The Secret Agent*. Roger Tennant (ed.). Oxford: Oxford University Press.

Conrad, Joseph (1984), *Nostromo*. Keith Carabine (ed.). Oxford: Oxford University Press.

Conrad, Joseph (1986), *The Collected Letters of Joseph Conrad: Volume 2: 1898–1902*. Frederick R. Karl and Laurence Davies (eds). Cambridge: Cambridge University Press.

Conrad, Joseph (1988), *Heart of Darkness* (3rd edn). Robert Kimbrough (ed.). New York and London: Norton.

Conrad, Joseph (1989), *'Heart of Darkness': A Case Study in Contemporary Criticism*. Ross C. Murfin (ed.). New York: St Martin's Press.

Conrad, Joseph (1995), *'Youth', 'Heart of Darkness', 'The End of the Tether'*. John Lyon (ed.). London: Penguin.

Conrad, Joseph (1996), *Heart of Darkness*. D. C. R. A. Goonetilleke (ed.). Ontario: Broadview.

Conrad, Joseph (2000), *'Heart of Darkness' with 'The Congo Diary'*. Robert Hampson (ed.). London: Penguin.

Conrad, Joseph (2002), *'Heart of Darkness' and Other Tales*. Cedric Watts (ed.). Oxford: Oxford University Press.

Conrad, Joseph (2006), *Heart of Darkness* (4th edn). Paul B. Armstrong (ed.). New York and London: Norton.

Davidson, John (1973), *The Poems of John Davidson*. Vol. 1. Andrew Turnbull (ed.). Edinburgh: Scottish Academic Press.

Dickens, Charles (1996), *Bleak House*. Nicola Bradbury (ed.). Harmondsworth: Penguin.

Defoe, Daniel (1986), *Robinson Crusoe*. Angus Ross (ed.). Harmondsworth: Penguin.

Eliot, George (1985), *The Mill on the Floss*. A. S. Byatt (ed.). Harmondsworth: Penguin.

Eliot, T. S. (2002), *Collected Poems 1909–1962*. London: Faber and Faber.

Ford, Ford Madox (1924), *Joseph Conrad: A Personal Remembrance*. London: Duckworth.

Ford, Ford Madox (1938), *Mightier Than the Sword*. London: George Allen and Unwin.

Ford, Ford Madox (1982), *Parade's End*. Robie Macauley (ed.). Harmondsworth: Penguin.

Ford, Ford Madox (1995a), *The Good Soldier*. Martin Stannard (ed.). New York and London: Norton.

Ford, Ford Madox (1995b), 'On impressionism', in Ford Madox Ford, *The Good Soldier*. Martin Stannard (ed.). New York and London: Norton, pp. 257–74.

Ford, Ford Madox (1999), *Return to Yesterday*. Manchester: Carcanet.

Ford, Ford Madox (2007), *It Was the Nightingale*. John Coyle (ed.). Manchester: Carcanet.

Haggard, H. Rider (1994), *King Solomon's Mines*. Harmondsworth: Penguin.

James, Henry (1966), *The Turn of the Screw*. Robert Kimbrough (ed.). New York and London: Norton.

James, Henry (1995a), *The Portrait of a Lady* (2nd edn). Robert D. Bamberg (ed.). New York and London: Norton.

James, Henry (1995b), 'Preface to the New York edition (1908)', in *The Portrait of a Lady* (2nd edn). Robert D. Bamberg (ed.). New York and London: Norton, pp. 3–15.

Joyce, James (2000), *A Portrait of the Artist as a Young Man*. Jeri Johnson (ed.). Oxford: Oxford University Press.

Joyce, James (2006), *Dubliners*. Margot Norris (ed.). New York and London: Norton.

Shakespeare, William (1972), *King Lear*. G. K. Hunter (ed.). Harmondsworth: Penguin.

Shakespeare, William (1995), *Twelfth Night, or What You Will*. Roger Warren and Stanley Wells (eds). Oxford: Oxford University Press.

Shelley, Mary (1992), *Frankenstein, or The Modern Prometheus*. Maurice Hindle (ed.). Harmondsworth: Penguin.

Stevenson, Robert Louis (2000), *The Strange Case of Dr Jekyll and Mr Hyde*. Martin A. Danahay (ed.). Ontario: Broadview.

Stoker, Bram (2000), *Dracula*. Glennis Byron (ed.). Ontario: Broadview.

Swift, Jonathan (1985), *Gulliver's Travels*. Peter Dixon and John Chalker (eds). Harmondsworth: Penguin.

Tolstoy, L. N. (1982), *War and Peace*. Rosemary Edmonds (trans.) Harmondsworth: Penguin.

Weissbort, Daniel (ed.) (1993), *The Poetry of Survival: Post-War Poets of Central and Eastern Europe*. Harmondsworth: Penguin.

SECONDARY TEXTS

Achebe, Chinua (1988), *Hopes and Impediments: Selected Essays 1965–1987*. Oxford: Heinemann.

Adams, Richard (1991), *Heart of Darkness*. Harmondsworth: Penguin.

Allen, Walter (1960), *The English Novel: A Short Critical History*. London: Phoenix House.

Ashcroft, Bill, Gareth Griffiths and Helen Tiffin (1995), *The Post-Colonial Studies Reader*. London: Routledge.

Ashcroft, Bill, Gareth Griffiths and Helen Tiffin (eds) (2002), *The Empire Writes Back: Theory and Practice in Post-Colonial Literatures* (2nd edn). London: Routledge.

Baines, Jocelyn (1993), *Joseph Conrad: A Critical Biography*. London: Weidenfeld & Nicolson.

Barthes, Roland (2000), 'The death of the author', in David Lodge and Nigel Wood (eds), *Modern Criticism and Theory: A Reader* (2nd edn). Harlow: Pearson Education.

Batchelor, John (1994), *The Life of Joseph Conrad: A Critical Biography*. Oxford: Blackwell.

Beckett, Samuel (1999), *Proust*. London: John Calder.

Bennett, Andrew, and Nicholas Royle (2004), *An Introduction to Literature, Criticism and Theory* (3rd edn). Harlow: Pearson Education.

Berthoud, Jacques (1978), *Joseph Conrad: The Major Phase*. Cambridge: Cambridge University Press.

Billy, Ted (1997), *A Wilderness of Words: Closure and Disclosure in Conrad's Short Fiction*. Lubbock: Texas Tech University Press.

Bloom, Harold (ed.) (1987), *Joseph Conrad's 'Heart of Darkness': Modern Critical Interpretations*. New York: Chelsea House.

Bonney, William W. (1980), *Thorns & Arabesques: Contexts for Conrad's Fiction*. Baltimore: Johns Hopkins University Press.

Bradbury, Nicola (1996), 'Introduction', in Charles Dickens, *Bleak House*. Nicola Bradbury (ed.). Harmondsworth: Penguin, pp. xi–xxvii.

Brantlinger, Patrick (1988), *Rule of Darkness: British Literature and Imperialism, 1830–1914*. Ithaca and London: Cornell University Press.

Brantlinger, Patrick (2004), 'Victorians and Africans: The genealogy of the myth of the dark continent', in Gene M.

Moore (ed.), *Joseph Conrad's 'Heart of Darkness': A Casebook*. Oxford: Oxford University Press, pp. 43–88.

Brooks, Peter (1992), *Reading for the Plot: Design and Intention in Narrative*. Cambridge, MA: Harvard University Press.

Burden, Robert (1991), *Heart of Darkness*. Basingstoke: Macmillan.

Carabine, Keith (ed.) (1992), *Joseph Conrad: Critical Assessments*. 4 vols. Mountfield: Helm Information.

Chantler, Ashley (1999), 'The Waltons: *Frankenstein*'s literary family'. *Byron Journal*, 27, 102–4.

Childs, Peter (2001), *Reading Fiction: Opening the Text*. Basingstoke: Palgrave.

Childs, Peter (2007), *Modernism and the Post-Colonial: Literature and Empire 1885–1930*. London and New York: Continuum.

Cixous, Hélène (1993), 'Sorties: out and out: attacks/ways out/forays', in Catherine Belsey and Jane Moore (eds), *The Feminist Reader: Essays in Gender and the Politics of Literary Criticism*. Basingstoke: Macmillan, pp. 101–16.

Coates, Paul (1988), *The Double and the Other: Identity as Ideology in Post-Romantic Fiction*. Basingstoke: Macmillan.

Collits, Terry (2006), *Postcolonial Conrad: Paradoxes of Empire*. London: Routledge.

Cox, C. B. (1974), *Joseph Conrad: The Modern Imagination*. London: J. M. Dent; Totawa, NJ: Rowman & Littlefield.

Cox, C. B. (ed.) (1982), *Conrad: 'Heart of Darkness', 'Nostromo' and 'Under Western Eyes'*. London: Macmillan.

Cuddon, J. A. (1991), *The Penguin Dictionary of Literary Terms and Literary Theory* (3rd edn). Harmondsworth: Penguin.

Dilworth, Thomas (1987), 'Listeners and lies in *Heart of Darkness*'. *Review of English Studies* (new series), 38.152, 510–22.

Docherty, Thomas (1983), *Reading (Absent) Character: Towards a Theory of Characterization in Fiction*. Oxford: Clarendon Press.

Esslin, Martin (1970), *The Theatre of the Absurd*. Harmondsworth: Penguin.

Feder, Lillian (1955), 'Marlow's descent into hell'. *Nineteenth-Century Fiction*, 9.4, 280–92.

Felman, Shoshana (1993), 'Women and madness: the critical

phallacy', in Catherine Belsey and Jane Moore (eds), *The Feminist Reader: Essays in Gender and the Politics of Literary Criticism*. Basingstoke: Macmillan, pp. 133–53.

Finkelstein, David (ed.) (2006), *Print Culture and the Blackwood Tradition, 1805–1930*. Toronto, Buffalo and London: University of Buffalo Press.

Fothergill, Anthony (1989), *Heart of Darkness*. Milton Keynes and Philadelphia: Open University Press.

Goonetilleke, D. C. R. A. (1990), *Joseph Conrad: Beyond Culture and Background*. Basingstoke: Macmillan; New York: St Martin's Press.

Greaney, Michael (2002), *Conrad, Language, and Narrative*. Cambridge: Cambridge University Press.

Greenslade, William (1994), *Degeneration, Culture and the Novel 1880–1940*. Cambridge: Cambridge University Press.

Griffith, John W. (1995), *Joseph Conrad and the Anthropological Dilemma*. Oxford: Clarendon Press.

Gross, Seymour L. (1957), 'A further note on the function of the frame in "Heart of Darkness"'. *Modern Fiction Studies*, 3, 167–70.

Guerard, Albert (1969), *Conrad the Novelist*. Cambridge, MA: Harvard University Press.

Gurko, Leo (1965), *Joseph Conrad: Giant in Exile*. London: Frederick Muller.

Hampson, Robert (1992), *Joseph Conrad: Betrayal and Identity*. Basingstoke: Macmillan; New York: St Martin's Press.

Hampson, Robert (2000), 'Introduction', in Joseph Conrad, *'Heart of Darkness' with 'The Congo Diary'*. Robert Hampson (ed.). London: Penguin, pp. ix–xliv.

Hartman, Geoffrey (2002), *Scars of the Spirit: The Struggle Against Inauthenticity*. Basingstoke: Palgrave Macmillan.

Hawkins, Hunt (1985), 'Conrad and the psychology of Colonialism', in Ross C. Murfin (ed.), *Conrad Revisited: Essays for the Eighties*. Alabama: University of Alabama Press, pp. 71–87.

Hawkins, Hunt (2006), '*Heart of Darkness* and racism', in Joseph Conrad, *Heart of Darkness* (4th edn). Paul B. Armstrong (ed.). New York and London: Norton, pp. 365–75.

Hawthorn, Jeremy (1979), *Joseph Conrad: Language and*

Fictional Self-Consciousness. Lincoln, NE: University of Nebraska Press.

Hawthorn, Jeremy (1992), *Joseph Conrad: Narrative Technique and Ideological Commitment.* London: Edward Arnold.

Hay, Elois Knapp (1979), 'Impressionism limited', in Norman Sherry (ed.), *Joseph Conrad: A Commemoration.* London: Macmillan, pp. 54–64.

Hewitt, John (1975), *Conrad: A Reassessment.* London: Bowes & Bowes.

Hyland, Peter (1988), 'The little woman in *Heart of Darkness*'. *Conradiana*, 20.1, 3–11.

Iser, Wolfgang (2000), 'The reading process: a phenomenological approach', in *Modern Criticism and Theory: A Reader* (2nd edn). David Lodge and Nigel Wood (eds). Harlow: Pearson Education, pp. 189–205.

Jefferson, Ann, and David Robey (eds) (1991), *Modern Literary Theory: A Comparative Introduction* (2nd edn). London: B. T. Batsford.

Johnson, Bruce (1985), 'Conrad's impressionism and Watt's "delayed decoding"', in Ross C. Murfin (ed.), *Conrad Revisited: Essays for the Eighties.* Alabama: University of Alabama Press, pp. 51–70.

Jones, Peter (ed.) (1972), *Imagist Poetry.* Harmondsworth: Penguin.

Jones, Susan (1999), *Conrad and Women.* Oxford: Clarendon Press.

Karl, Frederick R. (1979), *Joseph Conrad: The Three Lives: A Biography.* London: Faber and Faber.

Kermode, Frank (1991), *The Uses of Error.* London: Collins.

Knowles, Owen (1994), '"Who's afraid of Arthur Schopenhauer?": a new context for Conrad's *Heart of Darkness*'. *Nineteenth-Century Literature*, 49.1, 75–106.

Knowles, Owen, and Gene M. Moore (2006), *Oxford Reader's Companion to Conrad.* Oxford: Oxford University Press.

Kołakowski, Lesek (1999), *Freedom, Fame, Lying and Betrayal: Essays on Everyday Life.* Agnieszka Kołakowski. (trans.). Harmondsworth: Penguin.

Kolocotroni, Vassiliki, Jane Goldman and Olga Taxidou (eds) (1998), *Modernism: An Anthology of Sources and Documents.* Edinburgh: Edinburgh University Press.

Kundera, Milan (1996), *Testaments Betrayed*. Linda Asher (trans.). London: Faber and Faber.

Lawrence, D. H. (1998), *Selected Critical Writings*. Michael Herbert (ed.). Oxford: Oxford University Press.

Leavis, F. R. (1983), *The Great Tradition: George Eliot, Henry James, Joseph Conrad*. Harmondsworth: Penguin.

Levenson, Michael H. (1992), *A Genealogy of Modernism: A Study of English Literary Doctrine 1908–1922*. Cambridge: Cambridge University Press.

Lodge, David (1993), *The Modes of Modern Writing: Metaphor, Metonymy, and the Typology of Modern Literature*. London: Edward Arnold.

Lodge, David, and Nigel Wood (eds) (2000), *Modern Criticism and Theory: A Reader* (2nd edn). Harlow: Pearson Education.

Lyon, John (1995), 'Introduction', in Joseph Conrad, *'Youth', 'Heart of Darkness', 'The End of the Tether'*. John Lyon (ed.). London: Penguin, pp. vii–xlv.

McGann, Jerome J. (1998), *The Beauty of Inflections: Literary Investigations in Historical Method and Theory*. Oxford: Clarendon Press.

Maclean, Ian (1991), 'Reading and interpretation', in Ann Jefferson and David Robey (eds), *Modern Literary Theory: A Comparative Introduction* (2nd edn). London: B. T. Batsford, pp. 122–44.

McLeod, John (2000), *Beginning Postcolonialism*. Manchester: Manchester University Press.

Maier-Katkin, Birgit, and Daniel Maier-Katkin, (2004), 'At the heart of darkness: crimes against humanity and the banality of evil'. *Human Rights Quarterly*, 26, 584–604.

Matz, Jesse (2001), *Literary Impressionism and Modernist Aesthetics*. Cambridge: Cambridge University Press.

Meyers, Jeffrey (1991), *Joseph Conrad: A Biography*. London: John Murray.

Michael, Marion, and Wilkes Berry (1980), 'The typescript of *Heart of Darkness*'. *Conradiana*, 12.2, 147–55.

Middleton, Tim (2006), *Joseph Conrad*. London: Routledge.

Miller, J. Hillis (1985), '*Heart of Darkness* revisited', in Ross C. Murfin (ed.), *Conrad Revisited: Essays for the Eighties*. Alabama: University of Alabama Press, pp. 31–50.

Moore, Gene M. (ed.) (2004), *Joseph Conrad's 'Heart of Darkness': A Casebook*. Oxford: Oxford University Press.

Moser, Thomas (1957), *Joseph Conrad: Achievement and Decline*. Cambridge, MA: Harvard University Press; London: Oxford University Press.

Mulhern, Francis (2006), 'Conrad's inconceivable history'. *New Left Review*, 38, 59–93.

Murfin, Ross C. (ed.) (1985), *Conrad Revisited: Essays for the Eighties*. Alabama: University of Alabama Press.

Nadelhaft, Ruth L. (1991), *Joseph Conrad*. Hemel Hempstead: Harvester Wheatsheaf.

Najder, Zdzislaw (1997), *Conrad in Perspective: Essays on Art and Fidelity*. Cambridge: Cambridge University Press.

Najder, Zdzislaw (2007), *Joseph Conrad: A Life*. Haliner Najder (trans.). Rochester, NY: Camden House.

Parry, Benita (1983), *Conrad and Imperialism: Ideological Boundaries and Visionary Frontiers*. London: Macmillan.

Pater, Walter (1998) *The Renaissance: Studies in Art and Poetry*. Twickenham: Senate.

Peters, John G. (2003), *Conrad and Impressionism*. Cambridge: Cambridge University Press.

Raine, Craig (2000), *In Defence of T. S. Eliot*. London: Picador.

Ravel, Suresh (1986), *The Art of Failure: Conrad's Fiction*. Boston and London: Allen & Unwin.

Robbins, Ruth (2003), *Pater to Forster, 1873–1924*. Basingstoke: Palgrave Macmillan.

Roberts, Andrew Michael (ed.) (1993), *Conrad and Gender*. Amsterdam: Rodopi.

Roberts, Andrew Michael (2000), *Conrad and Masculinity*. Basingstoke: Macmillan; New York: St Martin's Press.

Robey, David (1991), 'Modern linguistics and the language of literature', in Ann Jefferson and David Robey (eds), *Modern Literary Theory: A Comparative Introduction* (2nd edn). London: B. T. Batsford, pp. 46–72.

Said, Edward W. (1968), *Joseph Conrad and the Fiction of Autobiography*. Cambridge, MA: Harvard University Press; London: Oxford University Press.

Said, Edward W. (1978), *Orientalism*. London: Routledge & Kegan Paul.

Sarvan, C. P. (1988), 'Racism in the *Heart of Darkness*', in Joseph Conrad, *Heart of Darkness* (3rd edn). Robert Kimbrough (ed.). New York and London: Norton, pp. 280–5.

Schwarz, Daniel R. (1980), *Conrad: 'Almayer's Folly' to 'Under Western Eyes'*. Basingstoke: Macmillan.

Selden, Raman, and Peter Widdowson (1993), *A Reader's Guide to Contemporary Literary Theory* (3rd edn). Hemel Hempstead: Harvester Wheatsheaf.

Sherry, Norman (1971), *Conrad's Western World*. Cambridge: Cambridge University Press.

Sherry, Norman (ed.) (1973), *Conrad: The Critical Heritage*. London: Routledge & Kegan Paul.

Sherry, Norman (ed.) (1976), *Joseph Conrad: A Commemoration*. London: Macmillan.

Showalter, Elaine (1990), *Sexual Anarchy: Gender and Culture at the Fin de Siècle*. London: Bloomsbury.

Simmons, Allan H. (2006), *Joseph Conrad*. Basingstoke and New York: Palgrave Macmillan.

Singh, Frances B. (1988), 'The colonialistic bias of *Heart of Darkness*', in Joseph Conrad, *Heart of Darkness* (3rd edn). Robert Kimbrough (ed.). New York and London: Norton, pp. 268–80.

Smith, Johanna M. (1989), '"Too beautiful altogether"': patriarchal ideology in *Heart of Darkness*', in Joseph Conrad, *'Heart of Darkness': A Case Study in Contemporary Criticism*. Ross C. Murfin (ed.). New York: St Martin's Press, pp. 179–98.

Spittles, Brian (1990), *How to Study a Joseph Conrad Novel*. Basingstoke: Macmillan.

Spittles, Brian (1992), *Joseph Conrad: Text and Context*. London: Macmillan.

Stape, J. H. (ed.) (2000), *The Cambridge Companion to Joseph Conrad*. Cambridge: Cambridge University Press.

Stape, J. H., and Owen Knowles (2006), 'Marlow's audience in "Youth" and "Heart of Darkness": a historical note'. *Conradian*, 31.1, 105–16.

Stern, J. P. (1985), *Nietzsche*. London: Fontana Press.

Stewart, Garrett (1980), 'Lying as dying in *Heart of Darkness*', in *PMLA*, 95.3, 319–31.

Stott, Rebecca (1996), *The Fabrication of the Late-Victorian Femme Fatale: The Kiss of Death*. Basingstoke: Macmillan.

Straus, Nina Pelikan (1987), 'The exclusion of the intended from secret sharing in Conrad's *Heart of Darkness*'. *Novel: A Forum on Fiction*, 20.2, 123–37.

Torgovnick, Marianna (2006), 'Primitivism and the African woman in *Heart of Darkness*', in Joseph Conrad, *Heart of Darkness* (4th edn). Paul B. Armstrong (ed.). New York and London: Norton, pp. 396–405.

Trilling, Lionel (1972), *Sincerity and Authenticity*. London: Oxford University Press.

Trotter, David (2000), *Cooking with Mud: The Idea of Mess in Nineteenth-Century Art and Fiction*. Oxford: Oxford University Press.

Valéry, Paul (1961), *The Art of Poetry*. Denise Folliot (trans.). New York: Vintage.

Veeser, H. Aram (ed.) (1989), *The New Historicism*. New York: Routledge.

Vidan, Ivo (1992), 'Conrad's legacy: the concern with authenticity in modern fiction', in Keith Carabine (ed.), *Joseph Conrad: Critical Assessments*. Vol. 4. Mountfield: Helm Information, pp. 396–413.

Watt, Ian (1974), 'Conrad's Preface to *The Nigger of the "Narcissus"*', in Joseph Conrad, *The Nigger of the 'Narcissus'*. Robert Kimbrough (ed.). New York: Norton, pp. 151–67.

Watt, Ian (1980), *Conrad in the Nineteenth Century*. London: Chatto & Windus.

Watts, Cedric (1977), *Conrad's 'Heart of Darkness': A Critical and Contextual Discussion*. Milan: Mursia International.

Watts, Cedric (1983), 'A bloody racist': about Achebe's view of Conrad'. *Yearbook of English Studies*, 13, 196–209.

Watts, Cedric (1984), *The Deceptive Text: An Introduction to Covert Plots*. Brighton: Harvester; Totowa: Barnes & Noble.

Watts, Cedric (1989), *Joseph Conrad: A Literary Life*. Basingstoke: Macmillan.

Watts, Cedric (1993), *A Preface to Conrad* (2nd edn). London: Longman; Harlow: Pearson Education.

Watts, Cedric (2000), 'Heart of Darkness', in J. H. Stape (ed.), *The Cambridge Companion to Joseph Conrad*. Cambridge: Cambridge University Press, pp. 45–62.

Wheeler, Michael (1990), *Death and the Future Life in Victorian Literature and Theology*. Cambridge: Cambridge University Press.

White, Allon (1981), *The Uses of Obscurity: The Fiction of Early Modernism*. London: Routledge & Kegan Paul.

Whitworth, Michael H. (ed.) (2007), *Modernism*. Oxford: Blackwell.

Wittgenstein, Ludwig (1955), *Tractatus Logico-Philosophicus*. Trans. C. K. Ogden. London: Routledge & Kegan Paul.

Woolf, Virginia (1966), *Collected Essays*. Vol. 2. London: Hogarth Press.

INDEX